ZAGAT SURVEY

Back in 1979, we never imagined that an idea born during a wine-fueled dinner with friends would take us on an adventure that's lasted three decades – and counting.

The idea – that the collective opinions of avid consumers can be more accurate than the judgments of an individual critic – led to a hobby involving friends rating NYC restaurants. And that hobby grew into Zagat Survey, which today has over 350,000 participants worldwide weighing in on everything from airlines, bars, dining and golf to hotels, movies, shopping, tourist attractions and more.

By giving consumers a voice, we – and our surveyors – had unwittingly joined a revolution whose concepts (user-generated content, social networking) were largely unknown 30 years ago. However, those concepts caught fire with the rise of the Internet and have since transformed not only restaurant criticism but also virtually every aspect of the media, and we feel lucky to have been at the start of it all.

As we celebrate Zagat's 30th year, we'd like to thank everyone who has participated in our surveys. We've enjoyed hearing and sharing your frank opinions and look forward to doing so for many years to come. As we always say, our guides and online content are really "yours."

We'd also like to express our gratitude by supporting **Action Against Hunger,** an organization that works to meet the needs of the hungry in over 40 countries. To find out more, visit www.zagat.com/action.

Nina and Tim Zagat

ZAGAT®
CELEBRATING 30 YEARS

Disneyland®
RESORT

Insider's Guide

Covering:
- **Attractions**
- **Dining**
- **Hotels**
- **Shopping**
- **Character Dining**

CONSULTING EDITOR
Laura Randall
STAFF EDITOR
John Deiner

Published and distributed by
Zagat Survey, LLC
4 Columbus Circle
New York, NY 10019
T: 212.977.6000
E: disney@zagat.com
www.zagat.com

ACKNOWLEDGMENTS

We thank Andrew Collins,
Bernard Onken and John
Rambow, as well as the following
members of our staff: Caitlin
Eichelberger (assistant editor),
Amy Cao (editorial assistant),
Brian Albert, Sean Beachell,
Maryanne Bertollo, Jane Chang,
Sandy Cheng, Reni Chin, Larry
Cohn, Alison Flick, Jeff Freier,
Andrew Gelardi, Roy Jacob,
Ashunta Joseph, Natalie Lebert,
Mike Liao, Dave Makulec, Andre
Pilette, Kimberly Rosado, Becky
Ruthenburg, Stacey Slate, Sharon
Yates, Anna Zappia
and Kyle Zolner.

Contents

Ratings & Symbols

Zagat Top Spot	Name		Zagat Ratings		
			CHILD	ADULT	THRILL
	⚡ Tim & Nina's Wild Ride		▽ 23	9	13

Details — Thrill Ride | Duration: 11 min | Wait: Moderate | Fastpass: Yes

Review, surveyor comments in quotes — "Reckless" thrill-seekers with "hearty" "appetites for adventure" climb aboard "catering trucks" for a "zigzagging" expedition into a "faux" Central Park, complete with "animatronic street musicians" and "angry squirrels"; prepare for "long lines" and "extended dizziness" – and "watch out for that jogger!"; P.S. "don't eat lunch" beforehand.

Ratings — Ratings cover key aspects of each category (e.g. Child Appeal, Adult Appeal and Thrill for Attractions). All are based on the Zagat 0 to 30 scale:

0	-	9	poor to fair
10	-	15	fair to good
16	-	19	good to very good
20	-	25	very good to excellent
26	-	30	extraordinary to perfection
	▽		low response	less reliable

Places without ratings are **newcomers** or **write-ins.**

Cost — **Attractions:** Included in park ticket; any additional fees are spelled out in reviews.

Dining: Reflects our surveyors' benchmark estimate of the price of dinner with one drink and tip.

Shopping: Indicated as I (inexpensive), M (moderate), E (expensive), VE (very expensive).

Hotels: Reflects high-season rate for a standard double.

Symbols

⚡ highest ratings, popularity and importance
◗ serves after 11 PM
B,L,D,S breakfast, lunch, dinner, snack

Top Lists and Indexes — Throughout Top Lists and Indexes, names are followed by their Disneyland Resort location. There is also a full Alphabetical index at the back of the book.

Helpful Information — We have included addresses and phone numbers with reviews only where it makes sense. For information on the Disneyland Resort, call 714-781-456 or visit www.disneyland.com.

About This Survey

This **Disneyland Resort Insider's Guide** is our first Survey of all that the classic California destination has to offer, including its two theme parks (**Disneyland** and **Disney's California Adventure**) and the **Downtown Disney District.** Covering attractions, dining, shopping and hotels, it offers advice on how to spend your time and money from thousands of people who've been there before you.

WHO PARTICIPATED: Input from 3,122 Disney-goers forms the basis for this guide's ratings and reviews (their comments are shown in quotation marks within the reviews). These surveyors are a diverse group: 66% are women, 34% men, while the breakdown by age is 17% in their 20s; 33%, 30s; 29%, 40s; 16%, 50s; and 5%, 60 and above. We thank each of these participants – this book is really "theirs." We are also grateful to the Walt Disney Co., which provided photos, maps and factual details.

HELPFUL LISTS: Whether you're a first-time visitor to the Disneyland Resort or a seasoned regular, our lists can help you make the right choices for you and your family. See the Top Ratings lists at the start of the sections for each park and Downtown Disney, as well as the 25 handy indexes starting on page 86. For Resort maps and photos – including a look at the Top 20 Thrills – see the color section at the back of the book.

ABOUT ZAGAT: This marks our 30th year reporting on the shared experiences of consumers like you. What started in 1979 as a hobby has come a long way. Today we have over 350,000 surveyors and now cover airlines, bars, dining, entertaining, fast food, golf, hotels, movies, music, resorts, shopping, spas, theater and tourist attractions in over 100 countries.

INTERACTIVE: Up-to-the-minute news about restaurant openings plus menus, photos and more are free on **ZAGAT.com** and the award-winning **ZAGAT.mobi** (for web-enabled mobile devices). They also enable reserving at thousands of places with just one click.

VOTE AND COMMENT: We invite you to join any of our surveys at **ZAGAT.com.** There you can rate and review establishments year-round. In exchange for doing so, you'll receive a free copy of the resulting guide when published.

AVAILABILITY: Zagat guides are available in all major bookstores as well as on **ZAGAT.com.** You can also access our content when on the go via **ZAGAT.mobi** and **ZAGAT TO GO** (for smartphones).

FEEDBACK: There is always room for improvement, thus we invite your comments about any aspect of our performance. Did we miss anything? Just contact us at **disney@zagat.com.**

New York, NY
January 12, 2009

Nina and Tim Zagat

What's New

Disneyland was the first of the Disney theme parks, having opened in 1955. Today it's adjoined by Disney's California Adventure and the Downtown Disney District. Together they inspire big-time devotion: the 3,122 surveyors who contributed to this guide – including many Anaheim locals – are frequent visitors, with 89% planning to return within the next six months. And lest you think it's just for kids, think again: 89% have visited without a child in tow – and 44% have gone solo.

TOWER OF POWER: We've rated each attraction separately for Adult and Child Appeal, and also included a Thrill rating for excitement hounds. With its score of 30 (the highest rating possible on the Zagat scale), the **Twilight Zone Tower of Terror** – a California Adventure standout featuring a plunge down an elevator shaft – ranks as the Resort's No. 1 Thrill and is also tops for Adult Appeal. Little ones prefer the **"Remember . . . Dreams Come True" Fireworks Spectacular,** a nightly extravaganza at Disneyland that's No. 1 for Child Appeal.

FUTURE INVESTMENT: An astonishing 15 million people passed through Disneyland's gates in 2007. Another 6 million made it to California Adventure; however, 90% of respondents prefer the original park to the 2001 addition. To remedy this situation, Disney is forging ahead on a $1.1 billion refurb: when completed in 2012, the park will be a vision of 1920s California. As part of the redo, **Toy Story Midway Mania!** opened in summer 2008 and instantly became one of the park's biggest draws (it ranks No. 2 for Child Appeal). In 2009, the **Sun Wheel** will be rethemed as **Mickey's Fun Wheel,** and some rides will disappear to make way for newcomers to be rolled out in the next few years – including the **World of Color,** a nightly water show near Paradise Pier; a **Little Mermaid** ride; and the 12-acre **Cars Land.**

NEW OPTIONS: Tinker Bell, whom 8% of our surveyors cited as their favorite Disney character (Mickey was No. 1, with 30% of the vote), has gotten her own Disneyland attraction: **Pixie Hollow,** a Fantasyland meet-and-greet that opened in fall 2008. The **Sleeping Beauty Castle Walkthrough** has reopened with enhanced effects.

EATING BETTER: Since 2006, menus at Disney parks have shifted toward healthier options; Disneyland's **French Market,** for instance, stopped serving fried chicken in mid-2008. Children's meals now include fruit or vegetables, vegetarian entrees are offered at table-service restaurants and both Resort parks have carts selling fresh produce. As for fine dining, many of the highest-rated restaurants for Food are in hotels, including the No. 1-ranked **Napa Rose** (Grand Californian) and the No. 2-ranked **Steakhouse 55** (Disneyland Hotel).

A REASON TO CELEBRATE: Budgeteers can save money in 2009 with the **"What will you celebrate?"** promotion, in which everyone who visits a Disney park on their birthday gets in for free. Other features include the daily Celebration Roundup barbecue in Disneyland and events like street parties.

New York, NY
January 12, 2009

John Deiner

A Disney Primer

WALT'S IT ALL ABOUT: Inspired by trips with his children to local carnivals, zoos and amusement parks, Walt Disney yearned to build a park that both children and adults would enjoy. That dream became a reality in July 1955, when **Disneyland** opened on a former orange grove with 27 rides and a $1 admission fee. It quickly became one of Southern California's top tourist attractions. It wasn't until 46 years later, in 2001, that the park expanded with the opening of **Disney's California Adventure** (also known as DCA) and the **Downtown Disney District,** a serpentine swath of shops and restaurants. These three areas are now collectively referred to as the Disneyland Resort.

LAY OF THE LAND: The Resort is located about 30 miles south of Downtown Los Angeles in Anaheim. It's possible (if exhausting) to cover both parks by foot and even sample Downtown Disney's offerings in a single day. The parks, with separate entrances across from one another, share parking lots and a shuttle drop-off area; Downtown Disney has its own parking lot but is within easy walking distance of the parks and the three Resort hotels: the **Disneyland Hotel, Disney's Grand Californian Hotel & Spa** and **Disney's Paradise Pier Hotel.**

SIBLING REVELRY: Think of Disneyland and Disney's California Adventure as siblings with wildly different looks and personalities. Disneyland – the bigger of the two, with some 48 rides as opposed to California Adventure's 25 – is the granddad of all theme parks, drawing large crowds and featuring attractions based on classic Disney characters. California Adventure pays homage to both the natural beauty and Hollywood glitz of the Golden State with a carnival-meets-wine-tasting vibe. Visitors tend to spend most of their time at Disneyland, though many use the smaller park as a midday respite from the other's bustle (for photos plus surveyor-based reviews of both parks, see page A2).

WHEN TO VISIT: Expect throngs from mid-July through August and mid-December through New Year's, especially at Disneyland. Spring break in late March or April also draws big numbers. Less-crowded months to visit are September, when kids are back in school, and January after the holidays (though you may find some rides closed for maintenance during these times). The parks go all out during Halloween and Christmas, with elaborate decorations and special events. Downtown Disney is at its liveliest on Friday and Saturday nights, when shops and restaurants stay open late.

WHAT IT COSTS: A single-day, one-park ticket is $69 for adults and $59 for ages three to nine (kids under three get in free). Many visitors prefer the one- or two-day **Park Hopper** ticket (one day, $94; two days, $143), which allows unlimited access to both Disneyland and California Adventure. You'll save between 10 and 20% on multiday Park Hopper tickets if you order online. Special after-hours events like Mickey's Trick-or-Treat Party in October are not included in the admission price. Guided tours, including the Walk in Walt's Footsteps Tour of Disneyland and the Cruzin' California Adventure Tour, also cost extra and require reservations (714-781-4400).

DINE TIME: Both parks offer a wide range of breakfast, lunch and dinner options, from food-cart churros and fresh fruit to sit-down table service, but most menus tend to be of the hamburger/pizza/turkey leg variety. Disneyland has more dining options than Disney's California Adventure, but the lines can be long at both during peak meal times, and reservations are a must at table-service restaurants, which generally close about one hour before their home parks do. Food and beverages from outside aren't allowed into the parks, but there is a picnic area to the west of the main Disneyland gate. Downtown Disney is also a good place to grab a bite, with more sit-down options and later hours (though these spots fill up quickly after the parks close). Call 714-781-3463 to book priority seating up to 60 days ahead at most Resort restaurants.

TIME SAVERS: Planning ahead will help you make the most of your visit. To experience the best of both parks in a single day, go to Disneyland first thing in the morning, when lines tend to be shortest, then head over to Disney's California Adventure in the afternoon to stroll Paradise Pier or catch a popular attraction like Soarin' Over California, and finish the day back in Disneyland for the nightly parade and more rides. Check www.disneyland.com a day or two ahead for show schedules and ride closures. At entrance gates, pick up a map and list of the day's events and show times and plot your itinerary. To avoid long waits for blockbusters like Disneyland's Space Mountain, pick up a free **Fastpass** at each ride's entrance as soon as you arrive; you'll get a ticket that gives you a designated time to return and lets you avoid the long standby line. Also, some attractions have **single-rider lines** that can cut wait times considerably. Parents may want to check out the **Rider Switch** program at attractions with height requirements. This lets one adult on the ride while the other one watches the child; at the ride's end, the other adult may board immediately.

GETTING THERE: The Resort is about 30 miles from LAX airport and 15 miles from the Orange County beaches of Laguna and Huntington; it's best to allow extra time during peak traffic periods. Those staying at hotels near the park can usually hop on a hotel- or city-operated shuttle, while drivers will be directed to the main Mickey & Friends lot, which offers covered parking for $12 a day. Parking in the separate Downtown Disney lot is free for the first three hours (or five hours with validation from a restaurant or AMC Theatres); there's also valet parking available in the evening.

KID CARE: Strollers are for rent ($12 a day) at both parks near the entrance gates. There's a first-aid station and baby care center, with diapers, toddler-size toilets and feeding areas, just beyond the photo shop on Main Street in Disneyland and next to the Mission Tortilla Factory in Disney's California Adventure. Bathrooms throughout the parks have changing tables.

ACCESSIBILITY: Most park attractions are wheelchair-accessible (maps available at the gate indicate which ones). Wheelchairs and motorized scooters are for rent for $12 and $45 a day, respectively, at both parks. Guests with disabilities may park in the first row of the Downtown Disney lot or in the Simba lot near the Paradise Pier Hotel. There's also a small drop-off area near the main gate where cars can park for 15 minutes or less.

Top-Rated Attractions

MOST POPULAR

1. Pirates of the Caribbean | *New Orleans Square, Disneyland*
2. Space Mountain | *Tomorrowland, Disneyland*
3. Soarin' Over California | *Golden State, DCA*
4. Indiana Jones Adventure | *Adventureland, Disneyland*
5. California Screamin' | *Paradise Pier, DCA*
6. Haunted Mansion | *New Orleans Square, Disneyland*
7. Big Thunder Mountain Railroad | *Frontierland, Disneyland*
8. Twilight Zone Tower of Terror | *Hollywood Pictures Backlot, DCA*
9. Buzz Lightyear Astro Blasters | *Tomorrowland, Disneyland*
10. Toy Story Midway Mania! | *Paradise Pier, DCA*
11. Splash Mountain | *Critter Country, Disneyland*
12. Fantasmic! | *Frontierland, Disneyland*
13. "Remember/Dreams Come True" Fireworks | *Disneyland*
14. Matterhorn Bobsleds | *Fantasyland, Disneyland*
15. Disney's Electrical Parade | *Parkwide, DCA*
16. "it's a small world" | *Fantasyland, Disneyland*
17. "Disney's Aladdin – Musical" | *Hollywood Pictures Backlot, DCA*
18. Peter Pan's Flight | *Fantasyland, Disneyland*
19. Enchanted Tiki Room | *Adventureland, Disneyland*
20. Jungle Cruise | *Adventureland, Disneyland*

BY THRILL RATING

30	Twilight Zone Tower of Terror	*Hollywood Pictures Backlot, DCA*
29	Space Mountain	*Tomorrowland, Disneyland*
	California Screamin'	*Paradise Pier, DCA*
28	Indiana Jones Adventure	*Adventureland, Disneyland*
27	Splash Mountain	*Critter Country, Disneyland*
	Grizzly River Run	*Golden State, DCA*
26	Maliboomer	*Paradise Pier, DCA*
	Matterhorn Bobsleds	*Fantasyland, Disneyland*
	Big Thunder Mountain Railroad	*Frontierland, Disneyland*
25	Soarin' Over California	*Golden State, DCA*
	"Remember/Dreams Come True" Fireworks	*Disneyland*
24	Toy Story Midway Mania!	*Paradise Pier, DCA*
23	Fantasmic!	*Frontierland, Disneyland*
2	Mulholland Madness	*Paradise Pier, DCA*
	Star Tours	*Tomorrowland, Disneyland*
1	Pirates of the Caribbean	*New Orleans Square, Disneyland*
	Sun Wheel	*Paradise Pier, DCA*
0	Haunted Mansion	*New Orleans Square, Disneyland*
	Mad Tea Party	*Fantasyland, Disneyland*
9	Buzz Lightyear Astro Blasters	*Tomorrowland, Disneyland*

BY ADULT APPEAL

29] Twilight Zone Tower of Terror | *Hollywood Pictures Backlot, DCA*
Space Mountain | *Tomorrowland, Disneyland*
California Screamin' | *Paradise Pier, DCA*
Soarin' Over California | *Golden State, DCA*
"Remember/Dreams Come True" Fireworks | *Disneyland*
Indiana Jones Adventure | *Adventureland, Disneyland*

28] Toy Story Midway Mania! | *Paradise Pier, DCA*
Fantasmic! | *Frontierland, Disneyland*
Grizzly River Run | *Golden State, DCA*
Big Thunder Mountain Railroad | *Frontierland, Disneyland*
Walk in Walt's Footsteps Tour | *Disneyland*
Splash Mountain | *Critter Country, Disneyland*
Pirates of the Caribbean | *New Orleans Square, Disneyland*

27] Matterhorn Bobsleds | *Fantasyland, Disneyland*
Haunted Mansion | *New Orleans Square, Disneyland*

26] Disney's Electrical Parade | *Parkwide, DCA*
"Disney's Aladdin – Musical" | *Hollywood Pictures Backlot, DCA*

25] Maliboomer | *Paradise Pier, DCA*
Buzz Lightyear Astro Blasters | *Tomorrowland, Disneyland*
Disneyland: First 50 Magical Years | *Main Street, Disneyland*

BY CHILD APPEAL

29] "Remember/Dreams Come True" Fireworks | *Disneyland*
Toy Story Midway Mania! | *Paradise Pier, DCA*
Buzz Lightyear Astro Blasters | *Tomorrowland, Disneyland*

28] Turtle Talk With Crush | *Hollywood Pictures Backlot, DCA*
Fantasmic! | *Frontierland, Disneyland*
Disney's Electrical Parade | *Parkwide, DCA*
Walt Disney's Parade of Dreams | *Parkwide, Disneyland*
Disney Princess Fantasy Faire | *Fantasyland, Disneyland*
Dumbo the Flying Elephant | *Fantasyland, Disneyland*
Mickey's House | *Mickey's Toontown, Disneyland*

27] Peter Pan's Flight | *Fantasyland, Disneyland*
Playhouse Disney | *Hollywood Pictures Backlot, DCA*
Autopia | *Tomorrowland, Disneyland*
Jedi Training Academy | *Tomorrowland, Disneyland*
Grizzly River Run | *Golden State, DCA*
Pixar Play Parade | *Parkwide, DCA*
Meet Pooh & Friends | *Critter Country, Disneyland*
Soarin' Over California | *Golden State, DCA*
Pirates of the Caribbean | *New Orleans Square, Disneyland*
"Disney's Aladdin-Musical" | *Hollywood Pictures Backlot, DCA*

Top-Rated Restaurants

TOP FOOD RATINGS BY CATEGORY

ADULT APPEAL
28 Napa Rose | *Grand Californian Hotel & Spa*
25 Steakhouse 55 | *Disneyland Hotel*
18 Blue Bayou | *New Orleans Square, Disneyland*

BREAKFAST
21 Catal | *Downtown Disney*
20 Storytellers Cafe | *Grand Californian Hotel & Spa*
19 Plaza Inn | *Main Street, Disneyland*

CAJUN/CREOLE
20 Ralph Brennan's Jazz Kitchen | *Downtown Disney*
19 Café Orleans | *New Orleans Square, Disneyland*
18 Blue Bayou | *New Orleans Square, Disneyland*

CALIFORNIAN
28 Napa Rose | *Grand Californian Hotel & Spa*
20 Storytellers Cafe | *Grand Californian Hotel & Spa*
19 Vineyard Wine Bar | *Golden State, DCA*

DESSERT
21 Gibson Girl Ice Cream Parlor | *Main Street, Disneyland*
20 Bur-r-r Bank Ice Cream | *Sunshine Plaza, DCA*
Main Street Cone Shop | *Main Street, Disneyland*

ENTERTAINMENT
20 Ralph Brennan's Jazz Kitchen | *Downtown Disney*
18 French Market | *New Orleans Square, Disneyland*
14 Tomorrowland Terrace | *Tomorrowland, Disneyland*

ITALIAN
19 Wine Country Trattoria | *Golden State, DCA*
18 Naples Ristorante e Pizzeria | *Downtown Disney*
17 Redd Rockett's Pizza Port | *Tomorrowland, Disneyland*

OUTDOOR DINING
21 Catal | *Downtown Disney*
19 Wine Country Trattoria | *Golden State, DCA*
Carnation Café | *Main Street, Disneyland*

PIZZA
18 Napolini | *Downtown Disney*
17 Redd Rockett's Pizza Port | *Tomorrowland, Disneyland*
15 Pizza Oom Mow Mow | *Paradise Pier, DCA*

SERVES ALCOHOL
19 Wine Country Trattoria | *Golden State, DCA*
Vineyard Wine Bar | *Golden State, DCA*
16 Uva Bar | *Downtown Disney*

VIEWS
28 Napa Rose | *Grand Californian Hotel & Spa*
19 Hook's Pointe | *Disneyland Hotel*
Wine Country Trattoria | *Golden State, DCA*

TOP DECOR RATINGS

27] Napa Rose | *Grand Californian Hotel & Spa*
26] Steakhouse 55 | *Disneyland Hotel*
25] Blue Bayou | *New Orleans Square, Disneyland*
Hearthstone Lounge | *Grand Californian Hotel & Spa*
23] Rainforest Cafe | *Downtown Disney*
Golden Horseshoe | *Frontierland, Disneyland*
22] Storytellers Cafe | *Grand Californian Hotel & Spa*
21] Ralph Brennan's Jazz Kitchen | *Downtown Disney*
Vineyard Wine Bar | *Golden State, DCA*
ESPN Zone | *Downtown Disney*

TOP SERVICE RATINGS

27] Napa Rose | *Grand Californian Hotel & Spa*
25] Steakhouse 55 | *Disneyland Hotel*
22] Yamabuki | *Paradise Pier Hotel*
21] Hearthstone Lounge | *Grand Californian Hotel & Spa*
Vineyard Wine Bar | *Golden State, DCA*
Hook's Pointe | *Disneyland Hotel*
Storytellers Cafe | *Grand Californian Hotel & Spa*
20] Blue Bayou | *New Orleans Square, Disneyland*
Catal | *Downtown Disney*
Wine Country Trattoria | *Golden State, DCA*

Top-Rated Shopping

MOST POPULAR

1. World of Disney | *Downtown Disney*
2. Emporium | *Main Street, Disneyland*
3. Build-a-Bear Workshop | *Downtown Disney*
4. Disneyana | *Main Street, Disneyland*
5. Candy Palace | *Main Street, Disneyland*
6. Disney's Pin Traders | *Downtown Disney*
7. Department 56 | *Downtown Disney*
8. Disney Clothiers LTD | *Main Street, Disneyland*
9. Pooh Corner | *Critter Country, Disneyland*
10. LEGO Imagination Center | *Downtown Disney*
11. Sephora | *Downtown Disney*
12. Greetings From California | *Sunshine Plaza, DCA*
13. Off the Page | *Hollywood Pictures Backlot, DCA*
14. Once Upon a Time/Princess Shoppe | *Fantasyland, Disneyland**
15. Star Trader | *Tomorrowland, Disneyland*
16. Indiana Jones Adventure Outpost | *Adventureland, Disneyland*
17. Marceline's Confectionery | *Downtown Disney*
18. Le Bat en Rouge | *New Orleans Square, Disneyland*
19. Mad Hatter Shop | *Main Street, Disneyland*
20. Adventureland Bazaar | *Adventureland, Disneyland*

TOP QUALITY RATINGS

28] Disneyana | *Main Street, Disneyland*
  Silhouette Studio | *Main Street, Disneyland*
  Off the Page | *Hollywood Pictures Backlot, DCA*
  Jewel of Orleans | *New Orleans Square, Disneyland*

27] China Closet | *Main Street, Disneyland*
  Marceline's Confectionery | *Downtown Disney*
  Disney's Pin Traders | *Downtown Disney*
  Portrait Artists | *New Orleans Square, Disneyland*
  Department 56 | *Downtown Disney*
  LEGO Imagination Center | *Downtown Disney*
  Disney Showcase | *Main Street, Disneyland*

26] Cristal d'Orleans | *New Orleans Square, Disneyland*
  World of Disney | *Downtown Disney*
  Build-a-Bear Workshop | *Downtown Disney*
  Disney Clothiers LTD | *Main Street, Disneyland*
  Candy Palace | *Main Street, Disneyland*
  Fossil | *Downtown Disney*
  Once Upon a Time/Princess Shoppe | *Fantasyland, Disneyland*
  Crystal Arts | *Main Street, Disneyland*
  Illuminations | *Downtown Disney*

* Indicates a tie with place above

DISNEYLAND PARK

Disneyland Park

A theme-park pioneer, Disneyland is similar but not identical to the Magic Kingdom, its larger sibling at Florida's Walt Disney World. It offers many of the same rides, plus a few unique ones – it's the only place in the Disney empire where you can zoom along on the **Matterhorn Bobsleds** or experience **Mr. Toad's Wild Ride.** It's also home to several of this Survey's winners, including the Most Popular Attraction (**Pirates of the Caribbean**) and the No. 1 for Child Appeal (**"Remember . . . Dreams Come True" Fireworks Spectacular**), as well as the Most Popular Restaurant (**Blue Bayou**). Regulars like to begin and end their day here, exiting for an afternoon jaunt to California Adventure or a nap in their hotel room.

HOURS: The park is generally open from 10 AM to 8 PM on weekdays and 8 AM to midnight on weekends. Visitors who buy multiple-day Park Hopper passes through the Disney website may enter the park an hour before it opens on select days (usually Sunday, Tuesday and Thursday); some attractions in Fantasyland and Tomorrowland are usually open during this window. Disney hotel guests may also be granted early access, but it depends on the season and crowd levels. Call ahead or check the website for hours.

PLANNING THE DAY: Disneyland is divided into eight sections. Most visitors start with a stroll down bustling **Main Street, U.S.A.,** then race to **Tomorrowland,** home of popular rides like **Autopia** and **Space Mountain** (note that height and age restrictions are posted at ride entrances and on maps available at the front gate; they're also shown in review headers where applicable). Afterward, they follow a generally counterclockwise path through **Fantasyland, Mickey's Toontown, Frontierland, Critter Country, New Orleans Square** and **Adventureland.** Those with flexible agendas, though, may want to hit Adventureland first, then go clockwise through the park, saving Tomorrowland for later in the day when crowds have thinned. Conserve energy by using the Disneyland Railroad to get from one section to another; it stops at Main Street, U.S.A., near the front gate, as well as New Orleans Square, Fantasyland and Tomorrowland. The monorail, with a station in Tomorrowland, is the fastest way to zip over to Downtown Disney.

CROWD CONTROL: Disneyland tends to be more crowded on weekends, when locals add to the mix of vacationers. Weekdays in the fall or late winter are often the quietest times. Consider entering the **single-rider** queue (available at some rides) or pick up a **Fastpass** for attractions like Autopia, **Splash Mountain** and Space Mountain so you can return later and avoid the long standby lines. Some rides only offer the Fastpass option on weekends. For popular rides that don't offer Fastpass, including the **Finding Nemo Submarine Voyage** and Pirates of the Caribbean, go in the morning or during parades. Check the Tip Board at the end of Main Street for estimated wait times, and pore over the guide to show times. Remember that some rides don't operate in poor weather or may be closed for refurbishment.

REFUELING: Convenience and variety characterize Disneyland dining, though park-goers tend to favor quick-service fare as they race from one attraction to another. Many of the options, whether carts, fast-food counters or sit-down restaurants, are themed to the section in which they're located: dine on jambalaya at Blue Bayou in New Orleans Square, dig into chicken breast nuggets and "Mile High" chocolate cake in air-conditioned comfort at the **Golden Horseshoe** in Frontierland or pick up kebabs at **Bengal Barbecue** in Adventureland. **Carnation Café** on Main Street is one of the few spots in either park that serves à la carte breakfast (highlights include Mickey-shaped waffles and coffee refills). Note that alcohol is not served anywhere in Disneyland.

BUY, BUY: Main Street, U.S.A., is a favorite place to stock up on all things Disney; it's anchored by the **Emporium,** piled high with clothes, toys and jewelry, and many of its merchants stay open an hour after the attractions close (they're often jam-packed with last-minute shoppers). Disneyland also has the best shops for pirate-themed clothes and toys (**Pieces of Eight**), dolls and princess costumes (**Once Upon a Time . . .**) and monogrammed Mouse ears (**Star Trader** and **Mad Hatter**). Disney hotel guests may request free delivery to their rooms, and all park-goers can bring their purchases to **Pioneer Mercantile** in Frontierland, Star Trader in Tomorrowland or the **Newsstand** near the entrance and have them held for pickup later. If you decide you want an item after you've left, call 800-362-4533 and describe it to a **DelivEars** operator who will track it down, process the purchase and arrange shipping (also applies to Disney's California Adventure).

Attractions

MOST POPULAR

1. Pirates of the Caribbean | *New Orleans Square*
2. Space Mountain | *Tomorrowland*
3. Indiana Jones Adventure | *Adventureland*
4. Haunted Mansion | *New Orleans Square*
5. Big Thunder Mountain Railroad | *Frontierland*
6. Buzz Lightyear Astro Blasters | *Tomorrowland*
7. Splash Mountain | *Critter Country*
8. Fantasmic! | *Frontierland*
9. "Remember/Dreams Come True" Fireworks | *Parkwide*
10. Matterhorn Bobsleds | *Fantasyland*

BY THRILL RATING

29| Space Mountain | *Tomorrowland*
28| Indiana Jones Adventure | *Adventureland*
27| Splash Mountain | *Critter Country*
26| Matterhorn Bobsleds | *Fantasyland*
Big Thunder Mountain Railroad | *Frontierland*
25| "Remember/Dreams Come True" Fireworks | *Parkwide*
23| Fantasmic! | *Frontierland*
22| Star Tours | *Tomorrowland*
21| Pirates of the Caribbean | *New Orleans Square*
20| Haunted Mansion | *New Orleans Square*

ADULT APPEAL

29| Space Mountain | *Tomorrowland*
"Remember/Dreams Come True" Fireworks | *Parkwide*
Indiana Jones Adventure | *Adventureland*
28| Fantasmic! | *Frontierland*
Big Thunder Mountain Railroad | *Frontierland*
Walk in Walt's Footsteps Tour | *Parkwide*
Splash Mountain | *Critter Country*
Pirates of the Caribbean | *New Orleans Square*
27| Matterhorn Bobsleds | *Fantasyland*
Haunted Mansion | *New Orleans Square*

CHILD APPEAL

29| "Remember/Dreams Come True" Fireworks | *Parkwide*
Buzz Lightyear Astro Blasters | *Tomorrowland*
28| Fantasmic! | *Frontierland*
Walt Disney's Parade of Dreams | *Parkwide*
Disney Princess Fantasy Faire | *Fantasyland*
Dumbo the Flying Elephant | *Fantasyland*
Mickey's House | *Mickey's Toontown*
27| Peter Pan's Flight | *Fantasyland*
Autopia | *Tomorrowland*
Jedi Training Academy | *Tomorrowland*

Dining

MOST POPULAR

1. Blue Bayou | *New Orleans Square*
2. Redd Rockett's Pizza Port | *Tomorrowland*
3. Café Orleans | *New Orleans Square*
4. Bengal Barbecue | *Adventureland*
5. Carnation Café | *Main Street*

TOP FOOD

19 Plaza Inn | *Main Street*
   Carnation Café | *Main Street*
   Café Orleans | *New Orleans Square*
18 Blue Bayou | *New Orleans Square*
   French Market | *New Orleans Square*

TOP FOOD (QUICK SERVICE)

21 Gibson Girl Ice Cream Parlor | *Main Street*
   Tiki Juice Bar | *Adventureland*
20 Little Red Wagon | *Main Street*
   Main Street Cone Shop | *Main Street*
   Critter Country Fruit | *Critter Country*

TOP DECOR RATINGS

25 Blue Bayou | *New Orleans Square*
23 Golden Horseshoe | *Frontierland*
21 Gibson Girl Ice Cream Parlor | *Main Street*
   Plaza Inn | *Main Street*
20 Tiki Juice Bar | *Adventureland*

TOP SERVICE RATINGS

20 Blue Bayou | *New Orleans Square*
19 Little Red Wagon | *Main Street*
   Carnation Café | *Main Street*
18 Plaza Inn | *Main Street*
   Main Street Fruit | *Main Street*

Shopping

Attractions

PARKWIDE

Discover the Magic Guided Tour
▽ 16 | 25 | 14

Tour | Duration: 2.5 hrs | Wait: n/a | Fastpass: No
Gain some "little-known", "behind-the-scenes" intel via this family-friendly parkwide outing as groups and their "knowledgeable" guides solve puzzles, match wits with baddies and ride six attractions in a process that "gives you a new perspective on the magic"; tours run Friday-Sunday, priced at $59 for the first two tickets and $49 each after that.

Holiday Time at Disneyland Guided Tour (Seasonal)
▽ 21 | 26 | 16

Tour | Duration: 3 hrs | Wait: n/a | Fastpass: No
"Priority seating for the Christmas parade" plus "cocoa and a cookie" are "bonuses" that help make this "enjoyable" tour through the "magical" holiday-season park "worth the price" ($59); groups also get VIP access to 'it's a small world' and the Haunted Mansion in their most festive form, as well as guides who let slip some "great trivia tidbits."

✷ "Remember . . . Dreams Come True" Fireworks Spectacular
29 | 29 | 25

Fireworks | Duration: 18 min | Wait: n/a | Fastpass: No
Ranked No. 1 for Child Appeal, this "jaw-dropping" "extravaganza" themed to the park's "main attractions" features "high-altitude pyrotechnics", a "laser show" and "Tinker Bell's flight", all "synchronized amazingly" to "thrilling music"; in sum, it's "the best fireworks show Disney's created" and the "ultimate way" "to top off the day" (that is, if it's not "canceled due to poor weather"); P.S. "try to position yourself" on Main Street with a "clear view of the castle and Matterhorn."

VIP Tour Services
▽ 18 | 25 | 16

Tour | Duration: n/a | Wait: n/a | Fastpass: No
"Expensive but well worth the money", this "incredibly helpful" service tailors your Disney experience via a personal guide's advice, stories, efficiently planned itineraries and general pampering; also providing prime seats at restaurants, shows and parades, it's "the way to go" even if all that dough ($750 for six hours, covering up to 10 guests) won't help you jump the line at any rides.

Walk in Walt's Footsteps Guided Tour
13 | 28 | 15

Tour | Duration: 3.5 hrs | Wait: n/a | Fastpass: No
"Full of behind-the-scenes secrets", this "entertaining and informative tour" features narration by Walt himself and includes a ride on the Railroad, priority entry into the Tiki Room and a "peek at the lobby of Club 33", the park's "exclusive" dining room; winding up with "a nice lunch" on Main Street, it's "perfect for Disney buffs" (though "a giant snore for children"); N.B. $59 per person.

Walt Disney's Parade of Dreams
28 | 24 | 16

Live Show | Duration: 35 min | Wait: n/a | Fastpass: No
"Only Disney could create" this "beautiful parade" down Main Street, an "uplifting" "visual and musical spectacle" that's "chock-full" of

"your favorite characters" "from past and present", doing an "amazing job" as they "seamlessly" "dance on and around" the "enchanting" movie-themed floats; adults will be "nostalgic" and "kids will be awe-struck", so "stake out a spot" and "get the cameras ready."

Welcome to Disneyland Guided Tour ▽ 18 | 24 | 14

Tour | Duration: 2.5 hrs | Wait: n/a | Fastpass: No
"The parks can be overwhelming" for "first-timers", so this "walking tour" puts "someone on your side" to deliver an "overview" of Disneyland and California Adventure over the course of an "informative" two-and-a-half-hour roving intro; along with "trivia" and "secrets", the $25 charge buys tips on using Fastpass and priority seating at a stage show or parade.

ADVENTURELAND

Enchanted Tiki Room 22 | 20 | 10

Animatronic Show | Duration: 13 min | Wait: Moderate | Fastpass: No
All the "singing birds and flowers" may have seemed "hokey" "even when it opened in 1963", but Adventureland's "tikilicious" "sit-down show" remains an "endearing" grab bag of "catchy tunes", "corny" jokes and "weirdly wonderful" "audio-animatronics"; if some flap that it's "too long", at least it's a "cool" "haven for a hot day", best enjoyed with a "refreshing" pineapple whip from the stand outside; P.S. the thunderstorm near the end "can be scary" for smaller kids.

☒ Indiana Jones Adventure 25 | 29 | 28

Thrill Ride | Duration: 4 min | Min ht: 46 | Wait: Very Long | Fastpass: Yes
"Hang on to your fedora" aboard Adventureland's "jaw-dropping" "dark ride on steroids", an "epic" 'jeep' "excursion" replete with "bumps, jostles and flames" to "get the adrenaline going"; the "dangers around every turn" "run the gamut" from "the world of Indy" ("poison darts", a "three-ton boulder", "snakes and skeletons") and are rendered in "amazing detail" that may be "too much for younger kids" – the "outrageous" lines are "a little scary" too.

Jungle Cruise 24 | 22 | 14

Boat Ride | Duration: 7 min | Wait: Moderate | Fastpass: No
"Familiarity never breeds contempt" for this "awesomely campy" Adventureland "tradition", an "easygoing" jungle tour aboard a "safari boat with a fearless guide" who "hams it up" with "corny wisecracks"; as long as your "skipper" has "comic timing", being "threatened by cannibals" and almost "eaten by piranhas" (part of a recent "update") "can make your day", but with a "lackluster guide" it can seem like one long "open-mike night."

Tarzan's Treehouse 21 | 12 | 10

Interactive Attraction | Duration: n/a | Wait: Short | Fastpass: No
"StairMasters have nothing on this" "reworking" of Adventureland's "sorely missed" Swiss Family Robinson tree house, now adapted to the "story of Tarzan and Jane"; beyond the "suspension bridge entrance" and "interactive play area", it's a "challenging climb" "with tweens running past you" up to the top, where the "workout" is rewarded with views "from on high."

CRITTER COUNTRY

Davy Crockett's Explorer Canoes

21 | 20 | 13

Boat Ride | Duration: 10 min | Wait: Moderate | Fastpass: No

This "old-school", "often-missed" Critter Country cruise uses "real canoes" steered by "witty" guides and "people-powered" by 20 guests "who have paddles but no clue how to use them"; "touring the Rivers of America" with Tom Sawyer Island "scenery" and "a little splashing" is an "enjoyable" "adventure", and "you'll have stronger arms" by the end; N.B. daytime only, usually in summer and on weekends.

Many Adventures of Winnie the Pooh, The

25 | 13 | 10

Car/Tram Ride | Duration: 3 min | Wait: Moderate | Fastpass: No

Pint-sized "Pooh fans rejoice" over this "delightful dark ride" in Critter Country, where guests board a "rolling beehive" for an "eye-catching" "journey through Hundred Acre Wood" that peaks in the "psychedelic dream-sequence room"; "young children can't get enough" of the "whimsy", but older folks have to bear with a jaunt that's "sticky sweet" yet "kind of blah"; P.S. it's "far off the beaten path", so the "line is usually pretty short."

Meet Winnie the Pooh & Friends

27 | 14 | 12

Interactive Attraction | Duration: n/a | Wait: Long | Fastpass: No

"Bring the kids and your patience" to this Critter Country meet-and-greet, an "organized mob scene" and "real time eater" that's nevertheless "a hit with little" fans granted "one-on-one time" (including an "autograph and photo op") with their "favorite Pooh characters"; although "they don't rush you", "cast members are there" to nudge "those who take a wee bit too long."

⚡ Splash Mountain

27 | 28 | 27

Flume/Whitewater | Duration: 8 min | Min ht: 40 | Wait: Very Long | Fastpass: Yes

"One hundred percent fun", this Critter Country "excursion" makes "a big splash" with "log flume" passengers who "drift" past "colorful scenery" and "singing animatronics" "themed to *Song of the South*" and "Br'er Rabbit's antics"; the journey's "gentle" until the "gnarly" "52-ft. final plunge" "into a very wet briar patch" – if you're up for "getting doused", it's a "fantastic way to cool off" "on a hot Zip-a-Dee-Doo-Dah day."

FANTASYLAND

Alice in Wonderland

26 | 18 | 10

Car/Tram Ride | Duration: 4 min | Wait: Moderate | Fastpass: No

"Follow the White Rabbit down the hole to awesomeville" aboard "cute" "pastel caterpillars" on this "classic dark ride" based on the 1951 'toon; though "super-long lines" make some Fantasylanders mad as a hatter, nostalgists say it's "worth the wait" to enjoy this "pleasant hallucination" featuring "lots of color and noise" plus "fabulous views" when the cars venture outside; be aware it can be "scary for toddlers."

Casey Jr. Circus Train

25 | 12 | 9

Train | Duration: 4 min | Wait: Moderate | Fastpass: No

It's easy to get "the toddler set" on board this "adorable" choo-choo "classic" of *Dumbo* fame for a "tour around Fantasyland" complete with a "bird's-eye view" of Storybook Land's "miniature towns and gardens" that's "truly Disney magic"; it may be a "long wait for such a short" trip, but it's a "nostalgic" favorite and "especially fun" to "ride locked in the monkey cage" – but only if you can "squish in" ("I think I can . . .").

Disney Princess Fantasy Faire
28 | 13 | 12

Interactive Attraction | Duration: n/a | Wait: Long | Fastpass: No
"Dreams come true for all little girls" at this "whimsical" Fantasyland "meet-and-greet" with a "plethora of princesses", where "coronations, dances at the maypole" and "storytelling" make "fairy-tale" interaction an "everyday treat"; just be sure "your wallet is thick" "if you start buying stuff", and expect "ridiculous wait times" for "photo ops" with the royals.

Dumbo the Flying Elephant
28 | 14 | 16

Spinning/Orbiting Ride | Duration: 2 min | Wait: Long | Fastpass: No
"Every kid" "has to ride" this "quintessential" Fantasyland fixture "at least once", as there's "nothing like getting an elephant's-eye view" while "soaring through the air" in "colorful" circling pachyderms that young aviators "maneuver" with "up/down controls"; as for adults, some "still love it", others "endure" it and all wish the "painfully long" lines didn't entail a "thrill-killer" wait ("pack a lunch").

"it's a small world"
26 | 19 | 10

Boat Ride | Duration: 12 min | Wait: Long | Fastpass: No
Like it or not, "you'll come out singing" the "cloying" yet "infectious" theme tune at this "essential" Fantasyland "staple" (revamped in 2008), one of the park's most "beloved" – if "repetitive" – rides; though "floating through a world" where "bobblehead dolls" "in multinational costumes" croon "in various languages" dismays "skeptics and grouches", "kids are mesmerized" and many older souls embrace its "honey-sweet innocence" "after all"; P.S. the "beautiful" "Christmas version" is "even better."

King Arthur Carrousel
26 | 15 | 12

Spinning/Orbiting Ride | Duration: 2 min 30 sec | Wait: Short | Fastpass: No
"Old-time, low-tech fun" for kids and "kids at heart", this "gorgeous carousel" in Fantasyland showcases "hand-carved" equines from the 19th century, painted panels with a "Sleeping Beauty theme" and a "classic" calliope soundtrack of Disney music; "the nostalgia factor" "never goes out of favor", and it's hard to find "anyone on this ride not smiling"; P.S. "look for the horse dedicated to Julie Andrews."

Mad Tea Party
26 | 22 | 20

Spinning/Orbiting Ride | Duration: 2 min | Wait: Moderate | Fastpass: No
A "real gigglefest" down to the "wobbly walk to the exit", this "iconic" Fantasyland "favorite" celebrating Alice in Wonderland's "happy unbirthday" is one "tea-riffic time" as riders in "colorful cups" madly spin the "center disk" "faster and faster" till "the world blurs"; the "dizzying" experience "never gets old", so "give it a whirl" if you can handle "having your breakfast scrambled" ("oh, my tummy!").

Matterhorn Bobsleds

24 | 27 | 26

Roller Coaster | Duration: 2 min 30 sec | Min ht: 35 | Wait: Very Long | Fastpass: No

This "landmark" Fantasyland coaster shoehorns you into a "cramped" bobsled that "whizzes through the depths" and peaks of a "mighty" "snowcapped" Alp, where a "Yeti with glowing eyes" awaits to make the trip suitably "hair-raising"; the "sudden dips and turns" are "bone-rattling" "compared to newer thrill rides", but most find it pure "exhilaration", down to the "splash-in-the-water finish."

Mr. Toad's Wild Ride

23 | 19 | 16

Car/Tram Ride | Duration: 2 min | Wait: Long | Fastpass: No

"Watch out for that train!": an "old-guard" Fantasyland dark ride that's still a "kick" "after more than 50 years", this "bizarre" but "adorable" "jaunt" croaks up "just the right amount of wildness" for most kids (toddlers may find it "kinda scary"); your "old-fashioned car" takes an "out-of-control" spin through Toad Hall and beyond, enduring "kooky" "twists and turns" until a "devilishly warm" finale that "makes no sense – but nobody seems to care" since it's such "a hoot."

Peter Pan's Flight

27 | 22 | 16

Car/Tram Ride | Duration: 2 min 30 sec | Wait: Very Long | Fastpass: No

Hooked "fans of Peter, Tink and Wendy" "never tire" of this "exemplary" Fantasyland "classic" from '55, which takes you "soaring" "through the stars" in a "pirate ship suspended from the ceiling", passing over the "twinkling lights" of London and "off to Never Land"; "beautiful, entrancing" and "timeless", it's "still unsurpassed for sheer heart" – and boasts "one of the park's longest lines" "to prove it" ("do this early").

Pinocchio's Daring Journey

22 | 16 | 12

Car/Tram Ride | Duration: 3 min | Wait: Short | Fastpass: No

"No lie", this dark "kiddie ride" in Fantasyland presents a "scenic" "re-telling" of the movie as Pinocchio "goes to Pleasure Island", "deals with Monstro the Whale" and winds up "back at home with the Blue Fairy, as a real boy"; but if it's "exciting" for children (and "too intense" "for toddlers"), adults who detect "nothing really daring" here hint the "line's short for a reason."

Pixie Hollow

- | - | -

Interactive Attraction | Duration: n/a | Wait: n/a | Fastpass: No

This Fantasyland meet-and-greet, which debuted in fall 2008 in what used to be Ariel's Grotto, is located along a twisty path lined with treelike blades of grass, bronze sculptures and other items designed to cut you down to pixie size; up ahead are Tinker Bell and her spritely friends, ready for photo ops and interaction with young fairies in training.

Sleeping Beauty Castle Walkthrough

- | - | -

Tour | Duration: n/a | Wait: n/a | Fastpass: No

Recently reopened after shuttering in 2001, this iconic walk-through returns with an overall look that's closer to the '50s original than it's been in decades; the storybooks and dioramas are now enhanced with computerized lighting and the latest effects, and new scenes give both the good fairies and the sinister Maleficent their due; N.B. a 'virtual' area allows those unable to navigate narrow halls and stairs to take part.

Snow White's Scary Adventures

| 20 | 15 | 13 |

Car/Tram Ride | Duration: 2 min | Wait: Moderate | Fastpass: No

"True to its name", this "incredibly dark" ride in Fantasyland "focuses on the scarier moments" of the "classic story", combining its tour of the dwarves' "adorable house" and a mine "sparkly with jewels" with "evil images" like the "wicked old" witch who "keeps popping up" "with a loud cackle"; it can be "frightening for children" and even "unsettling" for adults, right down to an "abrupt finish" with "no real happy ending."

Storybook Land Canal Boats

| 22 | 15 | 9 |

Boat Ride | Duration: 8 min | Wait: Long | Fastpass: No

This "corny" but "popular" guided boat ride is a Fantasyland "original" that glides "through Monstro the Whale's gigantic mouth" into a "beautifully crafted" "land of miniatures" with "bonsai landscaping" and "fairy-tale" scenery like "Cinderella's castle, the Three Little Pigs' houses and Aladdin's palace"; the "mellow" voyage is "enchanting" "for small children" but potentially a gigantic "snooze" for grown-ups (particularly after a "long wait in the hot sun").

Sword in the Stone Ceremony

| 23 | 14 | 11 |

Live Show | Duration: n/a | Wait: n/a | Fastpass: No

"Gather around the stone" nigh Fantasyland's King Arthur Carrousel for this periodic show, a "hokey but fun" enactment of the Excalibur legend wherein a "lucky" young "chosen one" gets a "chance to remove the sword" and be "crowned king for the day"; though hardly a "destination", it's good for "chuckles" as long as "Merlin is on his game."

FRONTIERLAND

Big Thunder Mountain Railroad

| 25 | 28 | 26 |

Roller Coaster | Duration: 3 min 30 sec | Min ht: 40 | Wait: Long | Fastpass: No

"Thrilling" but "not terror-inducing", this "family-friendly" "starter" coaster with "lots of turns and little tummy-tickler drops" is a "rootin', tootin'" Frontierland "classic"; riders "zoom through an Old West town" on a "runaway mine train" amid "highly detailed scenery", including "pitch-black tunnels" and "rocky caverns" – "keep your eye on the goat!" advise Thunder-heads, and "sit in the back" at night for the "wildest ride."

Big Thunder Ranch

| 19 | 14 | 7 |

Interactive Attraction | Duration: 10 min | Wait: None | Fastpass: No

"When it's open" (which is "rarely"), this "cute petting zoo" near Frontierland's Big Thunder Mountain coaster corrals "goats, sheep and a pretty cow" and is a "pleasant break from crowds" – "especially at holiday time", with "awesome decorations" plus "Santa and real reindeer"; "kids love it", but some adults empathize more with the "bored"-looking animals.

	CHILD	ADULT	THRILL

Fantasmic!   28 | 28 | 23

Live Show | Duration: 22 min | Wait: n/a | Fastpass: No

"A sensory feast", this "can't-miss" evening "extravaganza" staged on the Rivers of America "pulls out all the stops" with "pyrotechnics", live-action "swordfights", "a fire-breathing dragon", animation projected "on a water screen", villains "who scare all the children" and a "happy ending" courtesy of Mickey and other A-list heroes; go for the second, post-fireworks performance (if available) to avoid "camping out for hours" for a "decent spot."

Frontierland Shootin' Exposition   20 | 18 | 11

Arcade | Duration: n/a | Wait: n/a | Fastpass: No

Sharpshooters (i.e. "boys of all ages") "love the chance" to "show off" with "modified historic rifles" at this Frontierland "staple", sighting "electronic" guns on "Old West" targets "to trigger special effects"; a gun-shy minority takes aim at an "outdated" "waste of money", but loyalists insist it's "still the most fun 50 cents can buy."

Golden Horseshoe, The   18 | 25 | 12

Live Show | Duration: n/a | Wait: Moderate | Fastpass: No

Offering a "finger-snappin'", "toe-tappin'" "good time" in Frontierland's music hall, Billy Hill & the Hillbillies entertain with "virtuoso bluegrass mixed with rock 'n' roll and silly comedy"; it may be the "corniest thing in Disney", but the group's "fast-paced" stylings and "audience interaction" are a "hoot and a holler"; P.S. if the indoor snack bar's line is "long and slow", the outside window's is "always shorter."

Mark Twain Riverboat   17 | 20 | 9

Boat Ride | Duration: 15 min 30 sec | Wait: Moderate | Fastpass: No

"Smooth" and "majestic", this "authentic" "steam-powered" "paddle wheeler" cruising the Rivers of America offers a "chance to catch a breather" and "see Frontierland and New Orleans Square from the water"; "kids might be bored" by the "lazy ride", but to the "older generation" it's a "refreshing" "change of pace from the crowds"; P.S. "for an extra-special trip", "ask if it's possible to ride in the pilothouse."

Pirate's Lair on Tom Sawyer Island   27 | 18 | 14

Interactive Attraction | Duration: n/a | Wait: Short | Fastpass: No

"Aye matey", "photo ops" with "motley pirates" "await ye" at this "neat" "redo" of Frontierland's "old Tom Sawyer Island", now "upgraded" with "cool caves", bridges, tunnels and "treasures to be found around every corner"; "catch a raft" across the Rivers of America to reach the "wilderness" where "adults can rest" as their little scallywags "run, climb and crawl" "till they drop."

Sailing Ship Columbia   20 | 20 | 12

Boat Ride | Duration: 17 min | Wait: Moderate | Fastpass: No

Weighing anchor seasonally and "during peak days", Frontierland's full-size "replica" of an "18th-century" windjammer "takes leisurely", "picturesque" cruises on the Rivers of America; it's "neat" to "explore below decks" and "see how sailors lived", and it's "always an exciting moment" when they "fire the guns" – yet a few landlubbers will deem this voyage "ho-hum"; N.B. the vessel moonlights as the pirate ship in *Fantasmic!*

MAIN STREET, U.S.A.

Disneyland: The First 50 Magical Years
14 | 25 | 10

Movie/Multimedia | Duration: 13 min | Wait: n/a | Fastpass: No
Main Street's Opera House features a museum of Disneyana plus a "funny, breezy" film intro to the park that's "well worth watching" for "newcomers" and "enthusiasts" alike ("bonus: it's air-conditioned"); host "Steve Martin does a great job" narrating an "entertaining" Magic Kingdom history and "Donald Duck's antics" are a "quack-up", though the show can be "long for kids who'd rather be on a ride."

Disneyland Railroad
22 | 21 | 10

Train | Duration: 12 min 30 sec | Wait: Moderate | Fastpass: No
"All aboard!": this "genuine steam-powered train" is "not that exciting", but it's a "sentimental" "favorite" for many – and handy when "your feet are ready to fall off"; with four stops along the "rim of the park", the route includes a "long tunnel" between Tomorrowland and Main Street where an "old-timey" diorama of dinosaurs and the Grand Canyon provides a "cool" if "dated" glimpse of "animatronic kitsch."

Fire Engine, Main Street Vehicles
20 | 16 | 9

Car/Tram Ride | Duration: 3 min | Wait: n/a | Fastpass: No
"Riding any transport up and down Main Street is a blast", and that's especially true knowing that "Walt used to drive" this "open-air" replica of an early-1900s fire truck; ok, "it's not much of a thrill", but kids ("and some adults") "enjoy sitting in the very back" and "ringing the bell" during the "short (and slow)" trip.

Horse-Drawn Street Cars, Main Street Vehicles
20 | 19 | 10

Car/Tram Ride | Duration: 3 min 30 sec | Wait: n/a | Fastpass: No
"Some things never change", including the "relaxing, whimsical" rides on this trolley drawn by "big, powerful" horses; nostalgists say Main Street "just wouldn't be the same" without the "authentic", "old-time" feel they lend the area, plus the "friendly" drivers "know all the secrets" of the park; P.S. "if you're walking near these things, watch out."

Horseless Carriage, Main Street Vehicles
18 | 18 | 10

Car/Tram Ride | Duration: 2 min 30 sec | Wait: n/a | Fastpass: No
An "old-school" jaunt in this "open-air", canary-yellow replica of a 1903 vintage vehicle is "your chance to pretend" "you're important" as you "travel down Main Street" and "watch everyone get out of your way"; it may be "no adrenaline rush", but the "short, sentimental journey is as "much a part of Disneyland as Mickey Mouse."

Main Street Cinema
14 | 17 | 7

Movie/Multimedia | Duration: 3 min | Wait: None | Fastpass: No
With *Steamboat Willie* and five other "vintage" cartoons unreeling its "small screens", this seatless theater's "trip down memory lane" vibe "adds the right touch to Main Street", though for most "a brief walk-through suffices"; that it's "dark, cool and quiet" is a plus, but doubters wonder "why spend your time" taking in "primitive bits of art" "you could watch at home"?

Omnibus, Main Street Vehicles

18 | 17 | 8

Car/Tram Ride | Duration: 3 min | Wait: n/a | Fastpass: No
Holding 45 riders, this "old-time double-decker bus" with "chatty" drivers is a "cool" "change of pace" and offers welcome relief for "tired feet"; bonus: "stepping up" to the "upper deck" provides a "new view of Main Street."

MICKEY'S TOONTOWN

Chip 'n Dale Treehouse

20 | 5 | 6

Interactive Attraction | Duration: n/a | Wait: Short | Fastpass: No
"Kids seem to like" "climbing up and down" the "spiral staircase" inside this "simple" "playground piece" in a "far corner of Toontown", modeled on the chattering cartoon chipmunks' Redwood abode; otherwise there's "not much to it" ("anything fun was removed by lawyers a decade ago") other than "photo ops" and "a little sit-down time" for parents.

Donald's Boat

20 | 7 | 8

Interactive Attraction | Duration: n/a | Wait: None | Fastpass: No
"Chaotic" but "fun", this "short and sweet" Toontown "walk-through" lets "the little ones" "see how Donald Duck lives" at sea by exploring a "cute" two-tiered houseboat; they'll "blow off steam" as they "run up and down the stairs", "pretend to steer" and "honk the horn", but older salts say otherwise there's "not too much to do" on board.

Gadget's Go Coaster

27 | 15 | 19

Roller Coaster | Duration: 1 min | Min ht: 35 | Wait: Long | Fastpass: No
An "entry-level coaster for kids" that "still gives you that little rush", this "zippy" Toontown option ("cleverly themed" as a creation of *Chip 'n Dale Rescue Rangers*' resident inventor) features acorn-shell cars and a track that's a "contraption made of household objects"; it's "deceivingly fun", but given the "super-short" ride, "a long line isn't worth it."

Goofy's Playhouse

23 | 8 | 11

Interactive Attraction | Duration: n/a | Wait: n/a | Fastpass: No
Bringing Goofy's "wacky" "world to life", this Toontown "walk-through" lets "adults rest" as their "rambunctious" offspring "crawl all over" the house and "expend some energy" in the "tot lot", a "safely cushioned obstacle course"; it's beloved by "the five-and-under crowd", but some grown-ups grouse it's time to "rethink this one."

Mickey's House & Meet Mickey

28 | 17 | 14

Interactive Attraction | Duration: n/a | Wait: Long | Fastpass: No
"Little ones" "light up" "visiting the world's most famous mouse" at his "interactive" Toontown walk-through, a "darling" domicile outfitted with "clever" details and a "screening room" showing "vintage Mickey cartoons"; "be prepared to hurry up and wait" in "never-ending" lines for the "real payoff": a "short personal visit" with "the big cheese" himself for a hug, a "souvenir photo" and an autograph.

Minnie's House

26 | 15 | 11

Interactive Attraction | Duration: n/a | Wait: n/a | Fastpass: No
Favored by "younger girlie-girls who love everything pink, purple and cute", this "charming walk-through" in Toontown is "like stepping into cartoon" filled with "hands-on surprises" and "interactive appli-

ances" ("be sure to touch all the buttons and knobs in the kitchen"); the house "needs some TLC" after "so many guests", but "if you're lucky Minnie will be outside signing autographs."

Roger Rabbit's Car Toon Spin
24 | 20 | 18

Car/Tram Ride | Duration: 4 min | Wait: Long | Fastpass: Yes
"Enjoy the craziness" on this "dizzy", "garish" "interpretation of the film", a "lively" Toontown ride loaded with "kooky characters", "screwball sight gags" and "loud noises"; a "spinning car" you control "à la the teacups" "follows Roger and Jessica" through a "colorful and wacky" "cartoon" landscape where "laughs abound" "for all ages" - "just don't get carsick"; P.S. beware, the "line length is deceiving."

NEW ORLEANS SQUARE

Haunted Mansion
24 | 27 | 20

Car/Tram Ride | Duration: 6 min | Wait: Long | Fastpass: No
A "dark ride in more ways than one", this "must-do" "hallmark" of New Orleans Square oozes "tongue-in-cheek terror" as you "hop in a doom buggy" and explore a "spooky" manor where the "grim grinning ghosts come out to socialize"; it's "more amusing than scary" but still "might frighten" younger tykes; P.S. the "classic scenery is "souped up" for the holiday season with an "awesome" *Nightmare Before Christmas* makeover."

☑ Pirates of the Caribbean
27 | 28 | 21

Boat Ride | Duration: 16 min | Wait: Long | Fastpass: No
Voted the Survey's Most Popular Attraction, this "devilishly fun" "ride" inspired by a movie inspired by a ride" remains a New Orleans Square "must-do" that's "even more awesome" since an "update" added three "eerily lifelike" Jack Sparrows; after all, "who doesn't like" "watching debauchery on the high seas" from a "flume-style" boat that takes two "sudden drops" into the "amazingly detailed" realm of "animatronic pirates" who "plunder for treasure while singing a happy tune" – "yo ho!"

TOMORROWLAND

Astro Orbitor
25 | 16 | 16

Spinning/Orbiting Ride | Duration: 2 min | Wait: Moderate | Fastpass: No
In this "scarier older brother" of the Dumbo ride, Buzz Lightyear wannabes pilot rockets "around in circles" while "controlling their height" with a "push of a lever"; fans call it a Tomorrowland "keeper" with a "beautiful view" as bonus, but the "short" flight often comes with "long waits", the "uncomfortable" seating can be "difficult for tall adults" and those prone to motion sickness should "skip lunch" before launch.

Autopia
27 | 18 | 13

Car/Tram Ride | Duration: 5 min | Wait: Very Long | Fastpass: Yes
Kids can literally "drive their parents crazy" on this "revamped" "old favorite" in Tomorrowland that puts children "behind the wheel of a real car" on a "bumpy" track; petite Pettys proclaim it a "blast", but "insane" waits in the "unrelenting sun" and "slow-moving" vehicles

drain the batteries of many an adult; P.S. the gas pedal can be "difficult" to push without an "assist" from a "grown-up."

Z Buzz Lightyear Astro Blasters 29 | 25 | 19

Car/Tram Ride | Duration: 4 min | Wait: Long | Fastpass: Yes

"Blast those aliens!": in this "addictive" "interactive video game"/ride, everyone from "children to seniors" sits in "slow-moving" spinning cars and "gets out their inner geek" by "shooting at brightly colored targets" with "laser guns"; a few space cadets claim "some blasters work better than others", but the overwhelming buzz is that it's a "must-see"; P.S. e-mail kiosks let you send "photo evidence of your Astroblasting prowess" - a "cool" (and "rare") "Disney freebie."

Disneyland Monorail 20 | 20 | 10

Train | Duration: 11 min | Wait: Moderate | Fastpass: No

This "quaint" yet modern monorail - a vintage-1959 "vision of the future" - is a "smooth", "scenic way" to "whisk" between Downtown Disney and Tomorrowland that's "worth the wait if you've never done it" (bonus: ticket-holders boarding Downtown can bypass the park's "chaotic entrance" at opening time); it's "no longer a round trip", but it's still an "iconic Disney ride" and sure "beats walking."

Finding Nemo Submarine Voyage 26 | 18 | 14

Boat Ride | Duration: 17 min | Wait: Very Long | Fastpass: No

"Dive deeper and deeper" in a real lagoon as you "relive" the namesake movie in this "high-tech update" of Tomorrowland's "classic subs", where "Nemo and company" "come to life" via "impressive" "f/x" in a "colorful" "undersea adventure"; it's "popular" "with the smaller set", but elders are apt to find it "a claustrophobic underwhelm" after the "brutal" lines and "all the hype."

"Honey, I Shrunk the Audience" 20 | 18 | 14

Movie/Multimedia | Duration: 19 min | Wait: Moderate | Fastpass: No

An "interactive" "4-D show" combining a movie and "surprising" sensory effects, this "comedic" Tomorrowland "oldie" stars Rick Moranis as an absent-minded inventor who "accidentally shrinks" the audience down into prey for "crawling mice and slithering snakes" ("watch your toes!"); foes belittle a "stale" show that's "overdue for a change-out", but it still "makes you jump" - and can "scare some small kids."

Innoventions 16 | 17 | 8

Exhibit | Duration: n/a | Wait: Short | Fastpass: No

"The future is here, and it's air-conditioned" at this Tomorrowland pavilion that features "advertising-heavy displays" of "new technology" and "hands-on demonstrations at every turn"; but while some enjoy the "state-of-the-art gadgets", Honda's "neat" ASIMO robot and the "well-made" Dream Home, dissenters say it's just a "blah" "midday break" that could use a shot of innovention itself.

Jedi Training Academy 27 | 17 | 17

Live Show | Duration: n/a | Wait: Short | Fastpass: No

A "*Star Wars* fan's" "dream come true", this "totally cool" Tomorrowland interactive show selects "Jedis in the making" aged four to 12 from the audience to train and then "face off against Darth Vader and Darth Maul" in a "lightsaber duel"; the only downside is being "dis-

	CHILD	ADULT	THRILL

appointed when not chosen" – future Obi-Wans are usually pulled from the "front row", so "show up early" and "jump, wave and scream for attention."

⯌ Space Mountain
25 | 29 | 29

Roller Coaster | Duration: 3 min | Min ht: 40 | Wait: Very Long | Fastpass: Yes

Offering a "smoother" ride post-"refurb", this '70s-era Tomorrowland "favorite" remains a coaster "thrillathon" thanks to "wildly careening" "space shuttle" cars that "hurl you through" "a blackness" filled with "pulsating lights" and an "exhilarating soundtrack", keeping you "in constant suspense" over "which way the twists and turns will take you next"; though "the wait is forever", it's "beyond awesome" and possibly the best "in-the-dark experience you can have (legally)" at Disney.

Starcade
19 | 11 | 7

Arcade | Duration: n/a | Wait: n/a | Fastpass: No

"Bring quarters" and spend "a little downtime" at this video arcade near Space Mountain, which stars "some of the latest games" among a stable of 200; but while "teens and children" dig it, detractors ask "what's the point" of shouldering "extra cost" for an "outdated" "mall" amusement, especially when there are "rides to go on" ("get a life!").

Star Tours
24 | 25 | 22

Simulator | Duration: 5 min | Min ht: 40 | Wait: Long | Fastpass: No

"Nonstop excitement" awaits at this "space ride simulation" in Tomorrowland, a "moving theater" where the "bumpy journey" ("hold on tight") "to the moon of Endor" takes a "wild detour", leading into an "epic battle" against "the dreaded Death Star" "in a galaxy far, far away"; it may be "showing its age", but for *Star Wars* enthusiasts "this is still the closest you get to being in the movies."

Dining

ADVENTURELAND

Bengal Barbecue *American* 19 | 18 | 15 | $13

Counter service | L, D

"If you blink, you'll miss" this counter-service "hut" across from the Indiana Jones Adventure dishing up "messy" but "yummy" beef, chicken and vegetable skewers with "flavorful" sauces; sticklers sniff about "atrocious" lines and "limited" seating, but the majority deems it a "tasty bargain" that's "worth the wait."

Tiki Juice Bar *Dessert* 21 | 20 | 17 | $7

Counter service | S

"Set at the entrance to the Tiki Room" and its animatronic bird revue, this "little" Adventureland stand is a "must-do" for sweet-tooths craving "pineapple anything" – including "refreshing" juice, "creamy" "Dole whip" (a "swirl ice cream treat") and "heavenly" whip/juice floats; expect a "mile-long line", but when the show's over, you can't leave "without grabbing another."

Tropical Imports Fruit Cart *Health Food* ∇ 20 | 18 | 17 | $8

Food cart | S

Those "tired of junk food" and in need of something "to keep them going through Adventureland" can swing by this cart for a "healthy treat"; options include "fresh", "pre-sliced" fruit, "giant" pickles and "vegetable packs" – all "delicious", "no matter the time of year."

CRITTER COUNTRY

Critter Country Fruit Cart *Health Food* 20 | 14 | 18 | $8

Food cart | S

"Fresh fruit!" exclaim fiber-deprived folks who savor this Critter Country cart's "healthy" options while listening to "screaming riders on Splash Mountain"; advocates praise the likes of "tasty pineapple slices" and "crispy veggies", while sour grapes say it's "overpriced" and suggest "pack your own."

Hungry Bear Restaurant *American* 15 | 17 | 14 | $15

Counter service | L, D, S

"Watch the ships go by" while you nosh at this "open-air" "faux log cabin" in Critter Country with a "shady" bi-level terrace overlooking the Rivers of America; "fantastic" surroundings aside, the "basic" chow ("burgers, chicken sandwiches" and the like) is "kinda bland" and "pricey" and service can be "agonizingly slow"; P.S. kids can feed the "begging waterfowl."

FANTASYLAND

Enchanted Cottage *American* ∇ 16 | 18 | 18 | $15

Counter service | L, D, S

Bavarian-style brats, pretzels and chocolate-flavored popcorn are among the offerings at this counter-service cottage with a "cute" fairy-tale-inspired look; it's "not a bad choice" if visiting the nearby

Princess Fantasy Faire and 'small world' attractions, though a disenchanted few grump that you pay "a lot" for sauerkraut "out of a can" and "the same food" found everywhere else.

Fantasyland Fruit Cart *Health Food*

19 | 13 | 16 | $9

Food cart | S

"In a land of corn syrup and french fries", parents praise the "healthy" if "a tad expensive" "alternatives" (fruit, "trail mix or nuts", beverages) at this Fantasyland cart; with Snow White's Scary Adventures nearby, don't be surprised if you're tempted by the "giant apples."

Village Haus Restaurant *American*

14 | 18 | 14 | $14

Counter service | L, D

The "basic burgers and pizza" at this Fantasyland counter may be "run-of-the-mill" park fare, but "little ones" adore the setting: a "charming" "Bavarian-style" "cottage" bedecked with "quaint" murals depicting "Pinocchio's adventures"; pluses include its location near "many of the central rides" and "yodeling music that seems to quiet even the most fidgety kids."

FRONTIERLAND

Golden Horseshoe *American*

15 | 23 | 15 | $14

Counter service | L, D, S

"Hilarious" performances "will keep you laughing" at this "campy", "old saloon"–style Frontierland canteen, but the counter-service chow "doesn't match the show's quality"; despite applause for "excellent" chocolate cake and other desserts, the unimpressed deem the "mostly fried" "snacky stuff" (chicken breast nuggets, mozzarella sticks, etc.) just "ok", with "iffy" service.

Rancho del Zocalo *Mexican*

17 | 19 | 17 | $17

Counter service | L, D

At this "cafeteria-style" Mexican set behind an "inviting" faux Spanish facade in Frontierland, the "burritos are as big as your head"; amigos find the fare "surprisingly good" and appreciate the plentiful seating on a "lovely bougainvillea-covered patio", while a few foodies lament that given the SoCal locale, "it could be much better."

River Belle Terrace *American*

18 | 18 | 16 | $18

Counter service | B, L, D

"Mickey pancakes rule" at this "cafeteria-style" Frontierland icon providing "delicious", "filling" breakfasts (perhaps the "best in the park") and a "people-watching" patio "overlooking the Rivers of America"; while a 2007 refurb left the 1800s-style decor intact, a few loyalists decry the "revamped" American menu, now mostly "sandwiches and salads" instead of "good old-fashioned barbecue."

Stage Door Café *American*

16 | 15 | 15 | $12

Counter service | L, D, S

Serving the same satisfyingly "bad-for-you fried food" as the counter within Frontierland's Golden Horseshoe, this "hole-in-the-wall" outside the faux saloon dispenses "quick" fare like chicken tenders, fish 'n chips and "funnel cakes with three different toppings"; pluses include "outdoor seating" near the Rivers of America and an "always short line."

MAIN STREET, U.S.A.

Blue Ribbon Bakery *Bakery* | 19 | 17 | 17 | $11 |
Counter service | B, L, D, S
Near the park entrance, this "lovely", bustling Main Street "classic" sends diets "flying out the window" with such "decadent" treats as "giant" cookies and "scrumptious" cinnamon rolls, as well as specialty coffees and sandwiches "big enough to share" (making them "more cost friendly"); if only there were more "people behind the counter" to manage the "long lines."

Carnation Café *American* | 19 | 18 | 19 | $18 |
Table service | B, L, D
Dining "alfresco" beneath pink-and-white umbrellas at this "pleasant" Main Streeter offers harried park-goers an "escape from the crowds", but it's the American menu – "hearty" salads, sandwiches, "excellent" baked-potato soup – that has regulars returning "again and again"; "reasonable value" is a plus, and it's a "favorite" for breakfast ("Mickey waffles!"), hence there's "usually a line."

Gibson Girl Ice Cream Parlor *Ice Cream* | 21 | 21 | 17 | $9 |
Counter service | S
Dripping in "turn-of-the-century" ambiance, this "charming, old-fashioned" Main Street parlor wins kudos for its "elaborate sundaes", "fresh" "waffle cones that taste as good as they smell" and "generous scoops" of ice cream in "scrumptious" flavors; still, even enthusiasts gripe about "limited seating" and a "line as long as Space Mountain's."

Little Red Wagon *Hot Dogs* | 20 | 18 | 19 | $10 |
Food cart | L, D, S
"Mosey on up" to this "old red truck" doubling as an "outdoor vending cart" on Main Street for "ginormous", "amazing" corn dogs that "could feed two children easily"; throw in "chips and a drink" and you'll pay about 10 bucks – a deal "you can't beat."

Main Street Cone Shop *Ice Cream* | 20 | 16 | 17 | $8 |
Counter service | S
"Shh!" plead fans of this "hidden" Main Street "splurge" "near the lockers" where there's "never a long line" – just "old-fashioned hot-fudge sundaes" and "hand-dipped cones" with "generous" scoops of "yummy" ice cream jazzed up with "imaginative" toppings; still, even admirers gripe that it "needs to be open more often."

Main Street Fruit Cart *Health Food* | 19 | 15 | 18 | $8 |
Food cart | S
For a "quick pick-me-up", the Main Street masses can grab some "sweet, delicious" fruit at this cart near the park entrance where "everything is always fresh"; tables and chairs sit in the "peaceful" "little side alley" nearby, making it an altogether "nice place to pay too much for a light snack."

Plaza Inn *American* | 19 | 21 | 18 | $21 |
Counter service | B, L, D
One of Disneyland's "better bargains", this "family-friendly" Main Street "buffeteria" offers "humongous" servings of "hearty, home-

FOOD | DECOR | SERVICE | COST

style" American "comfort food" ("awesome" fried chicken, the "best pot roast ever") in a "quaint" "Victorian" setting; savvy regulars tout the patio for "watching the fireworks" and parades; P.S. "kids (and parents) love the character breakfasts" here.

Refreshment Corner *American* | 16 | 18 | 15 | $12

Counter service | S

Grab a "quick bite" from this Coca-Cola–themed counter-service eatery on Main Street, then "sit outside" and enjoy "good old ragtime music" performed by "piano players"; yes, the fare's "not thrilling" (hot dogs, Mickey-shaped pretzels and, natch, "homemade cherry Cokes"), but for nostalgic devotees of this circa-1955 landmark, "it all works" – right down to the "cracked marble flooring."

MICKEY'S TOONTOWN

Clarabelle's *American* | ∇ 16 | 19 | 17 | $12

Counter service | L, D, S

Look for the cow-patterned awning, then hoof it to this Toontown counter where a "friendly" staff dishes out "good frozen yogurt" and a choice of toppings; the "limited" offerings include sandwiches, salads, coffee drinks and ice cream bars.

Daisy's Diner *American* | ∇ 18 | 19 | 17 | $17

Counter service | L, D, S

Any way you slice it, this Daisy Duck–themed counter fits the bill for Toontowners hankering for "good pizza" ("veggie salad" too) served by a "fast, friendly" staff; it's a "favorite" of hatchlings, while adults appreciate the ample outdoor seating.

Pluto's Dog House *Hot Dogs* | 14 | 14 | 14 | $13

Counter service | L, D, S

"Every kid loves a hot dog", but not every parent digs this "no-thrills" wiener window; while most agree it's "not a bad bet" for "basic" fare among "Toontown's limited choices", a few state that, frankly, it's too "crowded" ("not what I would call Disney magic").

Toon Up Treats *American* | - | - | - | I

Counter service | S

Located in Toontown's City Hall area, this compact open-air counter attracts the hot dog- and pizza-weary; the self-service menu includes pickles, veggies, fruit, beverages and, for the decadent, apple slices with caramel sauce.

NEW ORLEANS SQUARE

☑ Blue Bayou *Cajun/Creole* | 18 | 25 | 20 | $39

Table service | Reservations: Required | L, D

At this "romantic" "escape from reality" – the Survey's Most Popular restaurant – diners "sit on a dock under stars" in the Pirates of the Caribbean launch area; fans call it a "must-do" for its Cajun-Creole fare ("order the Monte Cristo" at lunch) and dimly lit "New Orleans ambiance", and if scallywags snarl about a "limited" menu of "uninspiring", "overpriced" food, remember you're paying "for the setting" – and "it's so worth it"; P.S. book "far in advance."

	FOOD	DECOR	SERVICE	COST

Café Orleans *Cajun/Creole* | 19 | 19 | 17 | $21 |

Table service | Reservations: Required | B, L, D

The "cheap man's Blue Bayou", this waterside Cajun-Creole in New Orleans Square offers "many of the same items" as its popular sib – but at a "fraction of the price"; "interesting" breakfasts, "Mickey beignets" and "three-cheese Monte Cristos" earn kudos, but service can be "slow" and you're advised to "eat outside" for the "best atmosphere."

French Market *Cajun/Creole* | 18 | 19 | 16 | $19 |

Counter service | L, D

"Listen to jazz" and "enjoy the view" at this "reasonably priced" alfresco "buffeteria" in a New Orleans Square "garden setting"; serving "decent" Cajun-Creole, it's a "dependable" choice "if you can't get into" the swankier Blue Bayou, though some find the "long lines" unappetizing; P.S. a recent change to a healthier menu (not fully reflected in the Food rating) hasn't pleased everyone: "boo, no more fried chicken."

Mint Julep Bar *American* | 19 | 15 | 17 | $8 |

Counter service | S

"If you can find it" ("passholders don't even know" it's here), this "hidden gem" "near the railroad station" in New Orleans Square serves "refreshing" mint juleps and "must-try fritters"; sure, a few miss the booze ("what's the point?"), but more fret that the stand "is often closed."

Royal Street Veranda *Cajun/Creole*   ∇ | 19 | 14 | 15 | $13 |

Counter service | S

"When you're hankerin' for clam chowder in a bread bowl", high-tail it to this Cajun-Creole window "next to Pirates of the Caribbean" in New Orleans Square, a "great place for a quick bite"; "tasty" "steak or vegetable gumbo" and "fritters with dipping sauce" round out the menu.

TOMORROWLAND

Z Redd Rockett's Pizza Port *Pizza* | 17 | 15 | 15 | $15 |

Counter service | L, D

"Huge portions" of "mass-produced" but "tasty" pizza, pasta and salad at "reasonable prices" attract Tomorrowlanders to this "crowded" eatery "underneath Space Mountain"; "seating can be a challenge" and the "cafeteria-style" setup a "little hectic", but the "basic" Italian fare ("not bad, not great") includes enough choices "to make everyone happy."

Tomorrowland Fruit Cart *Health Food* | 18 | 12 | 17 | $7 |

Food cart | S

After a Space Mountain mission, avoid the "lines of insanity" at other Tomorrowland dining options by landing at this "healthy" cart across from the Star Trader shop; options include water, soft drinks and "fruit and vegetables" – "with no high-fructose corn syrup added", naturally.

Tomorrowland Terrace *American* | 14 | 13 | 14 | $14 |

Counter service | B, L, D, S

Space invaders who "score a table" overlooking the stage at this "crowded" Tomorrowland counter can "watch the Jedi Training Academy show" or "live bands" while they eat; otherwise, expect a "fair selection" of "unimaginative" fast food (listed on a "confusing menu display"), including "some healthy options" and "decent" breakfasts.

Shopping

ADVENTURELAND

Adventureland Bazaar
23 | 25 | 22 | M

Adventurelanders paw through *Lion King* toys, Paul Frank frocks and "all kinds of jungle-related stuff" at this "fun little" bazaar with "something for every budget"; boys dig the rubber snakes, girls "can become Princess Jasmine", and adults like that everything isn't "slapped with a Disney logo" and there are "shirts you'd actually wear in real life"; bonus: its less-trammeled home across from the Jungle Cruise ensures "more relaxed shopping."

Indiana Jones Adventure Outpost
24 | 25 | 23 | M

Adventure-seekers Jonesin' for "fedoras, whips" and "other Indy gear" will find their "dream place" across from the eponymous ride; there's "ample" space for checking out the "movie-style" clothes and accessories like "snakes, maps and action figures", but a few naysayers gripe about high prices and call the merch "kitsch for big kids."

South Sea Traders
25 | 25 | 25 | M

Wide-brimmed hats, grass skirts and "exotic gifts" pack a tropical punch at this tin-roofed Polynesian crowd-pleaser between Adventureland Bazaar and the Indiana Jones Adventure Outpost, where the moderately priced wares also include Disney-themed "surf-style shirts" and leis; N.B. look for Shrunken Ned, a British explorer who tells fortunes from behind a glass case for 50 cents a pop.

CRITTER COUNTRY

Pooh Corner
26 | 26 | 23 | M

"Who can resist Pooh?" ponder partisans of this "cuddly delight" of a toy shop near the Critter Country ride dedicated to the "bear of very little brain"; pluses include "items you won't find anywhere else" ("even gloomy Eeyore") and a remote cul-de-sac locale that makes it "never overly busy"; P.S. sweet tooths become piglets digging into "yummy" desserts at the adjoining Pooh's Hunny Spot.

FANTASYLAND

Disney Princess Fantasy Faire
24 | 26 | 23 | E

"Stock up on tiaras" and other princessabilia "until your eyes burn pink with sparkles" at this "wonderland" for pint-sized "fair maidens" across from the Toontown train station; face-painting and hair-styling are available too, as well as fantasy-themed toys, books and even swords and other gear for young knights.

Enchanted Chamber
- | - | - | M
(fka The Disney Castle Shoppe)

Tykes with wand-erlust flit into this Sleeping Beauty Castle nook in Fantasyland for all things Tinker Bell and fly out with midpriced T-shirts, costumes, handbags and jewelry; the pixie-resistant can pick through a smattering of princess-themed items like address books and tiaras; N.B. it recently changed its name from the Disney Castle Shoppe.

Fantasy Faire Gifts

24 | 25 | 25 | M

After their crowning achievements at the Disney Princess Fantasy Faire, rugrat royals pick through the plush toys, pins, lollipops and other small souvenirs that fill this nearby Fantasyland kiosk; meanwhile, camera-toters who've staked out a nearby spot for the nightly Parade of Dreams can stock up on supplies.

Heraldry Shoppe

24 | 26 | 23 | E

"Walk past the suit of armor" in Sleeping Beauty Castle into this "unique" shop whose "friendly" staff will help you explore the history of your family's name (if it's in the database), then "print out and mount" coats of arms on everything from T-shirts to wall hangings; the "great gift" options include rings and swords, but while partisans give it the seal of approval, a few crest-fallen consumers dub it "overpriced."

it's a small world Toy Shop

23 | 23 | 22 | M

Step off Fantasyland's 'it's a small world' and into a "traffic jam of major proportions" at this tiny cottage at the ride's exit; though most surveyors like the "cuddly stuffed animals", "dolls from all over" and Hot Wheels, the 'world'-weary bemoan the store's "limited" offerings and object to feeling "almost forced to walk through" it ("not cool").

Le Petit Chalet Gifts

▽ 25 | 25 | 22 | M

Nestled in the shadows of the Matterhorn, this Fantasyland kiosk carries a mountainous array of souvenirs and keepsakes, from character T-shirts to funky hats; if you prefer a different kind of foraging, "there's a turkey leg stand" nearby for biding time while your significant other "runs up the credit card."

Mad Hatter

26 | 25 | 23 | M

Like its Main Street sib, this chapeau depot near Fantasyland's Alice in Wonderland ride is filled to the brim with "hats galore", including "embroidered Mickey ears" and character visors; whether you "take pictures of friends in Goofy hats" or "go nutty" in a jester's cap, it'll "make you feel like a kid again"; P.S. personalize your purchase "at no extra charge."

Once Upon a Time,
The Disney Princess Shoppe

26 | 27 | 23 | E

"Your daughters will go nuts" in this "perfect little" Fantasylander attached to Sleeping Beauty Castle, where "princesses-to-be" find gowns, tiaras and jewelry representing "all the characters" (Belle, Ariel, etc.); though it "can get expensive quick", a "passionate" staff eases the pain, and "it's amusing to see the kids' hysteria" ("once upon a time, daddy couldn't possibly say no"); N.B. this shop will become the Bibbidi Bobbidi Boutique in April 2009.

Stromboli's Wagon

▽ 22 | 21 | 22 | M

No doubt your nose won't grow, but your mouth may water at the sight of this festively painted cart that's parked outside Pinocchio's Daring Journey in Fantasyland; it's chock-full of "cute stuff" like oversized lollipops and popcorn bags, plus basics such as small toys, postcards and key chains.

	QUALITY	DISPLAY	SERVICE	COST

Wishing Star
∇ 27 | 27 | 27 | E

(fka Three Fairies Magic Crystal Shop)
Near the exit of Pinocchio's Daring Journey, this softly illuminated cottage is filled with elegant displays of "amazing" crystal items that can be laser-engraved with two- or three-dimensional photographic images; N.B. the former Three Fairies Magic Crystal Shop, it was recently relocated from Sleeping Beauty Castle.

FRONTIERLAND

Bonanza Outfitters
25 | 25 | 25 | M

Next to Frontierland's Golden Horseshoe saloon, this "roomy" retailer wrangles an "abundance" of moderately priced Western-style shirts, sweaters and jackets for men and women, as well as pins and lanyards; N.B. collectors are hard-pressed to pass by the squished-penny machine near the exit.

Pioneer Mercantile
26 | 26 | 24 | M

"Davy Crockett hats", leather goods and all things Pocahontas (costumes, dolls, beanies) can be found at this "Western-themed" outpost just over the bridge to Frontierland; it's a "good stop" with kids, and prudent pioneers praise the "decent prices"; N.B. there's a pin-trading area in the back.

Silver Spur
- | - | - | M

Frontierland fun-seekers shuffle past a hulking wooden buffalo to round up the latest Disney apparel and accessories at this midpriced outpost next to Bonanza Outfitters; come November and December, it's stuffed with stockings, ornaments and other holiday items.

Westward Ho Trading Company
26 | 27 | 26 | M

Pin traders head over yonder to this rustic "little" merchant inside the Frontierland gate for its "wonderful" collection of pins and accessories and "well-informed" staff; meanwhile, sharp-dressed buckaroos laud the "good-quality" clothing with a "wide selection of character designs"; P.S. the holidays offer a stampede of "adorable Christmas ornaments."

MAIN STREET, U.S.A.

☑ Candy Palace
26 | 26 | 23 | M

"Sugar highs and childhood memories" rule at this Main Street "candy lover's treat" where you can watch fudge and other delectables "being handmade"; stock up on "gooey" sweets between attractions ("what is it about candy and thrill rides that go together?"), or take home "yummy" packaged confections; addicts swear by the English toffee ("to die for") and cinnamon candied apples, even if lines are "usually long."

Celebration Custom Printers
- | - | - | M

Let everyone know you're celebrating a birthday or other special occasion by donning personalized tees (buy a shirt, then pay by the line) from this new Main Streeter next to Disney Showcase; cast members can splash your name across a variety of designs, including Mickey and Minnie dressed as a bride and groom and Disney princesses; tip: Minnie, Goofy and other characters often gather outside the shop.

☑ China Closet
`27` `28` `26` `E`

"There's no bull in this china shop" on Main Street, just "fabulous ornaments", porcelain – "from Lladró to souvenir mugs" – and other "unusual Disney gift items"; "pleasant employees" and careful packaging ("they wrap your purchases like a mummy") round out the experience.

Crystal Arts
`26` `26` `24` `E`

Next door to Silhouette Studio on Main Street, this "sparkling adventure" features a big Sleeping Beauty Castle in its window and a "one-of-a-kind" selection of eye-catching, "somewhat costly" etched and cut glass, including "adorable" Disney figurines, mugs and jewelry, plus "fabulous" (and free) customized engraving; P.S. given all the breakables, "don't bring the kids in here."

☑ Disneyana
`28` `28` `27` `E`

Looky-loos and "die-hard collectors" alike "flock" to this "small" Main Street shop – No. 1 in the Survey for Quality – for its "excellent selection" of "high-end", "limited-edition" Disney collectibles, including animation cels, vintage ride posters and coffee-table books; prices can be "a bit high", so budgeteers treat it "more like a museum" and soak up the history lessons offered by the "knowledgeable" staff.

Disney Clothiers LTD
`26` `25` `24` `M`

Home to "fashionable" Disney duds "not found in other park stores", this popular Main Street vendor caters to "everyone in the family"; if the "nicely arranged" selection of "quality" shirts and PJs and "cute baby clothes" strikes some as a "bit pricey", most agree you can't beat its "quality and wearability."

Disney Showcase
`27` `26` `25` `E`

Disneyphiles praise the wide selection of Mouse-themed merchandise at this shop whose stock and styles "change frequently", making this a "fun stop as you travel up Main Street"; N.B. expect a bough-full of ornaments and holiday items in December.

☑ Emporium
`26` `26` `23` `M`

"How can you not stop in here!" shriek devotees of this "huge" "center of the Disney shopping universe" on Main Street; it's a "kitsch" catch-all with "just about everything you've seen" parkwide (shirts, magnets, mugs, etc.) at "every price range", plus window displays "like Saks in NYC during Christmas"; P.S. "avoid the mad rush" following the fireworks "unless you like people standing on top of you."

Fortuosity Shop
`–` `–` `–` `E`
(fka New Century Timepieces)

Formerly New Century Timepieces, this newly refurbed boutique is adjacent to Main Street's Emporium and carries a variety of jewelry and gifts, from frames and key chains to porcelain cups and Tinker Bell T-shirts; carried over from the old shop are "incredible, collectible" clocks and made-to-order Disney watches.

Mad Hatter Shop, The
`25` `25` `25` `M`

The topperati tip their "Mouse ears" to this "small" corner "classic" on Main Street that fans dub Disneyland's "best hat shop"; the "creative" caps range from "princess crowns" to "Disney logo" headgear, but most park-goers fall head over heels for the iconic Mickeywear (with "instant customization" by a "friendly" staff); P.S. it's sometimes "less crowded" than its Fantasyland counterpart.

Main Street Magic Shop
22 | 23 | 26 | M

"Budding illusionists" make money disappear at this "classic" magic shop on Main Street that carries "inexpensive" "gags and dime-store tricks", plus "some real professional equipment" (to be "perplexed and amazed", ask a cast member for a demonstration); P.S. star-gazers like to point out that "Steve Martin got his start" here.

Main Street Photo Supply Co.
25 | 21 | 23 | E

Whether you need "camera accessories, memory cards or film", "out-standing" cast members snap to it at this "hectic" photog's favorite at the castle end of Main Street; it's also the "place to pick up your pic-tures from the rides you've been on."

Market House
▽ 29 | 26 | 24 | E

The aroma of brewing java and a pot-bellied stove dominate this "always busy" Main Street stalwart where you can pick up Mickey's "Really Swell" joe, gourmet pasta and kitchen supplies; or grab a chair and enjoy the "refillable cups of coffee" and barbershop quartet serenades.

New Century Jewelry
▽ 27 | 26 | 27 | E

Sharing an entry with the Fortuosity Shop, this recently remodeled Main Streeter offers "moderate to expensive" costume and fine jewelry (including gold charms) that's a "cut above"; the decor is more Victorian parlor – chandeliers, wallpaper, sparkling glass cases – than workaday emporium, an ambiance abetted by the "helpful, patient" staff.

Newsstand
21 | 20 | 21 | I

The last store you pass before exiting Disneyland, this tiny "old-fashioned newsstand" is ideal for "fast" last-minute purchases (post-cards, film, magnets, etc.); it's also the pickup point for purchases made throughout the park that you didn't want to lug around.

ⓩ Silhouette Studio
28 | 23 | 28 | M

"Watch the scissors fly" while sitting for an "amazing" "Victorian sil-houette" in this "small" Main Street "gem" – "an original Disneyland tradition" that "everyone should do once" (you can also pose with a friend or add a Disney character); if cutups contend that "this gets more expensive as the years pass", most agree it's "just as cool."

20th Century Music Company
23 | 21 | 21 | M

For "a wide variety" of "hard-to-find" Disney music, books and DVDs, check out this "little shop on Main Street"; loyalists especially appre-ciate the soundtracks "specific to Disneyland shows and rides", though a few gripe that some items "can be found cheaper at your lo-cal store"; P.S. employees will "look up any Disney movie and tell you when it was last released and when it may be released again."

MICKEY'S TOONTOWN

Gag Factory – Toontown Five & Dime
24 | 25 | 23 | M

A "cool" spot for the "joker in the family", this "always entertaining" Toontowner tickles "every age" with its "nicely displayed" selection of affordable magic tricks, gadgets and T-shirts featuring Mickey and Co.; creative types swoon over the new "design-your-own Mouse ears" section – "even if they're mostly directed toward girls."

NEW ORLEANS SQUARE

Cristal d'Orleans
26 | 27 | 25 | E

Deemed "a delight for the eyes", this New Orleans Square shop boasts a "beautiful" (if "a bit expensive") selection of high-quality crystal and glass with "something for everyone's taste", from hand-blown glassware to chandeliers and paperweights ("bought our wedding cake topper here"); N.B. have a mug engraved and observe the in-house glassblower at work while you wait.

⊠ Jewel of Orleans
28 | 27 | 28 | VE

Some tout this "hidden gem" nestled in a New Orleans Square alley as one of the "best shops in Disneyland", specializing in pricey, "one-of-a-kind" estate jewelry (rings, brooches); even wallet-watchers find it's "worth a walk-through", thanks to "friendly" service and "beautiful" displays – "you may even find a piece Captain Jack doesn't have."

Le Bat en Rouge
25 | 26 | 24 | M

A "dream" for "Jack Skellington fans", this "charmingly creepy" boo-tique in New Orleans Square has "everything for the *Nightmare Before Christmas*" aficionado, including costumes, purses, clothes and jewelry; not surprisingly, it's a spook-tacular spot for "Halloween decor", though a few wish there were "more collectibles" and "Haunted Mansion–related" items.

L' Ornement Magique
26 | 25 | 24 | E

It's Christmas "every day" in this "tiny" mart across from New Orleans Square's Blue Bayou restaurant; the halls are decked with "out-of-the-ordinary" "glass ornaments with a Disney flair" and other Mouse-themed decor, but some find prices "a bit high" and the space a bit tight – "you can feel like a bull in a china shop."

Parasol Cart
25 | 24 | 24 | M

The "neat" purple, pink and white parasols from this cart next to Cafe Orleans in New Orleans Square make "one-of-a-kind" keepsakes for belles-in-the-making; but don't rush off, y'all: cast members will paint names, flowers and other designs on them while you wait.

Pieces of Eight
23 | 24 | 21 | M

"Get yer pirate loot" at this "overflowing" cave next to Pirates of the Caribbean; swashbucklers swoon over the "treasures and trinkets for all ages", including swords, eye patches and hats (all the "yo-ho-yo but no bottles of rum"), while a few mateys mutter it's "crowded" and plead "arr, cut the prices now, won't ye?"

Portrait Artists
27 | 25 | 27 | E

At this alfresco "treasure", "wonderful" artists "capture the spirit of" their subjects as they pose on a quiet New Orleans Square *rue*; satisfied customers crow that the finished products turn out "far beyond expectations" and become family keepsakes ("I still have my drawing from 1959").

	QUALITY	DISPLAY	SERVICE	COST

Royal Street Sweepers   - | - | - | M

A "sugar rush" awaits at this cart in New Orleans Square across from the Rivers of America; besides lollipops and other sweet treats, the Technicolor display includes souvenir glow necklaces, Mardi Gras masks and feather boas.

TOMORROWLAND

Autopia Winner's Circle   - | - | - | M

Mini drivers revved up by their Autopia jaunt pull into this pit stop near the attraction's entrance ramp to stock up on auto-themed trinkets, including model cars based on the ride, keychains and checkered flags; N.B. this was formerly the home of the Hatmosphere shop.

Little Green Men Store Command   24 | 24 | 22 | M

"You'll swear you're seeing little green men" when you touch down at this well-themed Tomorrowland outpost, which "pin traders" pointedly insist has the park's "best collectible pin selection"; its location at the exit of the Buzz Lightyear Astro Blasters ride means you'll also find "lots of cute Pixar things" and "all your Buzz needs" ("my kids always want to buy the gun or the aliens").

Star Trader   25 | 24 | 21 | M

Darth Vader meets Donald Duck at this "excellent" Tomorrowlander at the Star Tours exit; fans call it "second only to the Emporium" for Disney clothes and souvenirs, with extras like "build-your-own light sabers" and "realistic" photos of you as Han Solo or Princess Leia; the dark side: it can be "crowded" and prices are a "bit high", especially for "exclusive" *Star Wars* fare.

Tomorrowlanding   21 | 22 | 21 | M

After catching a show at the Jedi Training Academy stage, budding knights can snap up *Star Wars* merchandise (light sabers, shirts, Jedi Mickey) at this tiny vendor across from Innoventions in Tomorrowland; if the Force isn't with you, pore over the Goofy and Pluto hats and *Finding Nemo* knickknacks instead.

DISNEY'S CALIFORNIA ADVENTURE PARK

Disney's California Adventure Park

Home to the **Twilight Zone Tower of Terror** (the Survey's No. 1 Attraction for Adult Appeal and Thrill factor), **Disney's California Adventure** opened in 2001 as a hip homage to the Golden State. It began a four-year renovation in 2008 that will reflect California in the '20s – when Walt Disney arrived – and include several new major attractions. Be aware that the park is in a state of flux, with many attractions, shops and restaurants affected by the upcoming changes.

HOURS: The park typically opens at 10 AM and closes at 6 PM on weekdays and 8 PM on weekends. It stays open later during the busier summer and holiday seasons and days when Disneyland closes early for private events. Call ahead or check the website for hours.

PLANNING THE DAY: It's possible to cover the park in a day, though plan ahead to hit all the highlights. Begin a visit at **Sunshine Plaza,** where Mickey and Minnie are often on hand to pose for photos, then head to **Golden State** – you'll find **Grizzly River Run** and one of this Survey's most popular rides, **Soarin' Over California,** which debuted here (a version has since been added to Disney World's Epcot). Afterward, continue on to **Paradise Pier,** where you can ride the high-speed **California Screamin'** coaster and the new **Toy Story Midway Mania!,** a combination dark ride/shooting gallery that keeps track of your score. This is also home to the **Sun Wheel,** a 150-ft. Ferris wheel featuring regular cars, as well as cabins that swing wildly on tracks when the ride rotates (its new incarnation as Mickey's Fun Wheel will be unveiled in spring '09). Then head to **"a bug's land,"** where the preschool set appreciates the puddle park and gentle attractions. Finish up at the **Hollywood Pictures Backlot,** with the Tower of Terror and the Broadway-style *Disney's Aladdin - a Musical Spectacular.* Note that height and age restrictions are posted at ride entrances and on maps available at the front gate; they're also shown in review headers where applicable.

CROWD CONTROL: To minimize wait times, pick up a **Fastpass** for the Tower of Terror and Soarin' Over California as soon as you arrive, then make a beeline for Toy Story Midway Mania!, a Fastpass-free attraction that opened in summer 2008 whose lines get longer as the day progresses. Also consider jumping on a **single-rider queue** (available at some rides). Don't forget about the **Rider Switch** program, popular with parents of younger children. Available at major attractions with height requirements, it allows one adult to go on the ride while the other stays with the child; afterward, the waiting adult boards without rejoining the queue. And factor in show times when planning your visit: for instance, folks start lining up about an hour beforehand for *Aladdin - a Musical Spectacular* and 30 minutes ahead for *Playhouse Disney - Live on Stage!* Ask about show schedules and attraction wait times at the booth outside **Engine Ears Toys** near the park entrance.

REFUELING: Park diners are, for the most part, limited to quick-service options such as food carts and counter-service eateries, including the **Pacific Wharf Café** in Golden State, whose outdoor food court and views of Paradise Bay make it a favorite lunch stop. For sit-down service, park-goers can head to Golden State's **Wine Country Trattoria,** which overlooks the **Pixar Play Parade route.** Unlike Disneyland, alchohol is available at a few spots, including the **Cove Bar** on Paradise Pier.

BUY, BUY: California Adventure can't match Disneyland in terms of retail offerings, but its shops are fun to browse, with beach or boardwalk themes and inventory that focuses less on Mickey and more on Pixar and other Mouse franchises. **Treasures in Paradise,** for example, stocks *High School Musical* merch, Engine Ears is known for its build-your-own Mr. Potato Head area and the **Studio Store** in the Hollywood Pictures Backlot specializes in Muppets and *Monsters, Inc.* knickknacks. At **Rushin' River Outfitters** in Golden State, drenched park-goers can purchase a dry T-shirt after getting doused on the nearby Grizzly River Run raft ride (particularly handy in cooler weather). Disney hotel guests can request free delivery to their rooms, and all park-goers can bring their purchases to Engine Ears and have them held for pickup later in the day. For information on the park's shopping options, call 800-362-4533.

CAL. ADVENTURE

Attractions

MOST POPULAR

1. Soarin' Over California | *Golden State*
2. California Screamin' | *Paradise Pier*
3. Twilight Zone Tower of Terror | *Hollywood Pictures Backlot*
4. Toy Story Midway Mania! | *Paradise Pier*
5. Disney's Electrical Parade | *Parkwide*
6. "Disney's Aladdin – Musical" | *Hollywood Pictures Backlot*
7. Grizzly River Run | *Golden State*
8. Animation Academy | *Hollywood Pictures Backlot*
9. Turtle Talk With Crush | *Hollywood Pictures Backlot*
10. Monsters, Inc. Mike & Sulley Rescue | *Hollywood Pictures Backlot*

BY THRILL RATING

- 30 Twilight Zone Tower of Terror | *Hollywood Pictures Backlot*
- 29 California Screamin' | *Paradise Pier*
- 27 Grizzly River Run | *Golden State*
- 26 Maliboomer | *Paradise Pier*
- 25 Soarin' Over California | *Golden State*
- 24 Toy Story Midway Mania! | *Paradise Pier*
- 22 Mulholland Madness | *Paradise Pier*
- 21 Sun Wheel | *Paradise Pier*
- 19 Orange Stinger | *Paradise Pier*
- 18 It's Tough to Be a Bug! | *"a bug's land"*

ADULT APPEAL

- 29 Twilight Zone Tower of Terror | *Hollywood Pictures Backlot*
  - California Screamin' | *Paradise Pier*
  - Soarin' Over California | *Golden State*
- 28 Toy Story Midway Mania! | *Paradise Pier*
  - Grizzly River Run | *Golden State*
- 26 Disney's Electrical Parade | *Parkwide*
  - "Disney's Aladdin – Musical" | *Hollywood Pictures Backlot*
- 25 Maliboomer | *Paradise Pier*
- 24 Animation Academy | *Hollywood Pictures Backlot*
- 22 It's Tough to Be a Bug! | *"a bug's land"*

CHILD APPEAL

- 29 Toy Story Midway Mania! | *Paradise Pier*
- 28 Turtle Talk With Crush | *Hollywood Pictures Backlot*
  - Disney's Electrical Parade | *Parkwide*
- 27 Playhouse Disney | *Hollywood Pictures Backlot*
  - Grizzly River Run | *Golden State*
  - Pixar Play Parade | *Parkwide*
  - Soarin' Over California | *Golden State*
  - "Disney's Aladdin – Musical" | *Hollywood Pictures Backlot*
- 26 Redwood Creek Trail | *Golden State*
  - Monsters, Inc. Mike & Sulley Rescue | *Hollywood Pictures Backlot*

Dining

MOST POPULAR

1 Taste Pilots' Grill | *Golden State*
2 Wine Country Trattoria | *Golden State*
3 Corn Dog Castle | *Paradise Pier*
4 Bur-r-r Bank Ice Cream | *Sunshine Plaza*
5 Award Wieners | *Hollywood Pictures Backlot*

TOP FOOD RATINGS

<u>20</u> Bur-r-r Bank Ice Cream | *Sunshine Plaza*
   Boudin Bread Cart | *Golden State*
   Farmer's Market Fruit | *Golden State*
<u>19</u> Sam Andreas Shakes | *Golden State*
   Wine Country Trattoria | *Golden State*

TOP DECOR RATINGS

<u>21</u> Vineyard Wine Bar | *Golden State*
   Wine Country Trattoria | *Golden State*
<u>18</u> Taste Pilots' Grill | *Golden State*
   Pizza Oom Mow Mow | *Paradise Pier*
<u>17</u> Bur-r-r Bank Ice Cream | *Sunshine Plaza*

TOP SERVICE RATINGS

<u>21</u> Vineyard Wine Bar | *Golden State*
<u>20</u> Wine Country Trattoria | *Golden State*
<u>19</u> Boudin Bread Cart | *Golden State*
<u>17</u> Farmer's Market Fruit | *Golden State*
   Bur-r-r Bank Ice Cream | *Sunshine Plaza*

CAL. ADVENTURE

Shopping

MOST POPULAR

1 Greetings From California | *Sunshine Plaza*
2 Off the Page | *Hollywood Pictures Backlot*
3 Engine Ears Toys | *Sunshine Plaza*
4 Rushin' River Outfitters | *Golden State*
5 Gone Hollywood | *Hollywood Pictures Backlot*

TOP QUALITY RATINGS

28| Off the Page | *Hollywood Pictures Backlot*
25| Greetings From California | *Sunshine Plaza*
　 Engine Ears Toys | *Sunshine Plaza*
　 Gone Hollywood | *Hollywood Pictures Backlot*
24| P.T. Flea Market | *Golden State*

TOP DISPLAY RATINGS

28| Off the Page | *Hollywood Pictures Backlot*
26| Engine Ears Toys | *Sunshine Plaza*
25| Greetings From California | *Sunshine Plaza*
24| Gone Hollywood | *Hollywood Pictures Backlot*
　 P.T. Flea Market | *Golden State*

TOP SERVICE RATINGS

26| Off the Page | *Hollywood Pictures Backlot*
24| Gone Hollywood | *Hollywood Pictures Backlot*
　 Greetings From California | *Sunshine Plaza*
23| P.T. Flea Market | *Golden State*
　 Rushin' River Outfitters | *Golden State*

Attractions

PARKWIDE

Cruzin' Disney's California Adventure Park! Tour ▽ | 16 | 24 | 18 |
Tour | Duration: 3 hrs | Wait: n/a | Fastpass: No
When you're ready to roll, "it's worth" getting up at "o'dark o'clock" and paying a "pricey" $99 for this three-hour "behind-the-scenes" Segway tour around California Adventure "before the gates open"; after a "light breakfast" and "some instruction" on the gizmo (it's "a lot easier than it looks"), you have "the run of the park" – it's "sooo cool."

Disney's Electrical Parade | 28 | 26 | 17 |
Live Show | Duration: n/a | Wait: n/a | Fastpass: No
An "eye-popping" California Adventure "highlight", this "classic" nighttime "spectacle" showcasing "light-encrusted floats" and a "glittering" "procession of Disney characters" is "amazing to behold"; with a "wonderful blaze" of color and "upbeat" "electronic music" that "sticks in the head for days", it's "a real crowd-pleaser" "that never gets old"; P.S. parades are seasonal and not held every day, so "check time listings" beforehand.

High School Musical 3: Senior Year: Right Here! Right Now! | - | - | - |
Live Show | Duration: n/a | Wait: n/a | Fastpass: No
Go Wildcats!: this performance in the streets of California Adventure includes six songs taken from the third *HSM* movie; it's a high-energy show whose strength is a hard-working cast skilled at getting onlookers to join in all the singing, dancing and tween-oriented excitement.

Pixar Play Parade | 27 | 22 | 17 |
Live Show | Duration: n/a | Wait: n/a | Fastpass: No
"Upbeat music", "colorful floats" and "random water sprays" ("watch out!") "generate squeals of delight" as this "high-energy, bubble-filled" "winner of a parade" proceeds through California Adventure's Sunshine Plaza; along for the "interactive" ride are "cute" "Pixar stars" ("the Incredibles, Nemo, Buzz and Woody", etc.), suggesting this one might "turn into a classic" if the studio "keeps churning out hits."

A BUG'S LAND

Bountiful Valley Farm | 14 | 12 | 5 |
Interactive Attraction | Duration: 20 min | Wait: None | Fastpass: No
Families seeking "no-thrills" downtime in 'a bug's land' can buzz over to this "spread-out" exhibit and "learn a little" about California agriculture; kids soak up the "wonderful" "water play area" where they can "get wet on a hot day", but naysayers find it all "about as much fun as watching lettuce grow"; N.B. the ongoing park refurb means this attraction will be buying the farm.

Flik's Flyers, Flik's Fun Fair | 25 | 13 | 14 |
Spinning/Orbiting Ride | Duration: 1 min 30 sec | Wait: Short | Fastpass: No
"Made just for" "the preschooler set", this "whimsical" draw in 'a bug's land' is akin to "Dumbo without the wait", with riders boarding

"giant Chinese take-out boxes" and snack containers that "swirl" "up and then around" a "pie-tin" axis; though it's "a little dizzying", every "adventurous" tot will want to "give it a spin."

Francis' Ladybug Boogie, Flik's Fun Fair | 24 | 13 | 14

Spinning/Orbiting Ride | Duration: 1 min 30 sec | Wait: Short | Fastpass: No
California Adventure's "slower", "smaller-scale" "twist on the teacups" concept appeals to "younger" explorers of 'a bug's land' with "cute" ladybug-shaped cars spinning in "herky-jerky" "figure eights" and nearly bumping at intersections; it's on the "tamer" side, but with "few toddler attractions" to choose from, "this one's a hit" with half-pints.

Heimlich's Chew Chew Train, Flik's Fun Fair | 22 | 9 | 7

Train | Duration: 1 min 30 sec | Wait: Short | Fastpass: No
"Toddlers and the pre-K crowd" make tracks to this "short" ride in 'a bug's land', where "Heimlich the caterpillar" trains "munch" their way through a "gigantic garden" filled with "smell-o-vision" scents like "watermelon and animal crackers"; fed-up elders find it "too cute" and say you should "only chew choose this" "snooze" "if your child insists."

It's Tough to Be a Bug! | 24 | 22 | 18

Movie/Multimedia | Duration: 8 min 30 sec | Wait: n/a | Fastpass: No
"Expect surprises" and "be prepared to use all your senses" at this "funny" "audio-animatronics show" in 'a bug's life', an "interactive" "4-D adventure" that "makes you feel you've been shrunk down to ant size" and then sends "giant" insects "at you from every direction"; it's "downright entertaining", but even the most bug-eyed fans agree this one's "way too intense for young kids."

Princess Dot Puddle Park, Flik's Fun Fair | 26 | 11 | 13

Interactive Attraction | Duration: n/a | Wait: n/a | Fastpass: No
"Have a change of clothes handy" at this splashy playground in 'a bug's land', a "chaotic" oasis of "water fun" where "sprinklers shoot" every which way and "your kids have the time of their lives getting soaked"; it's "not for unprepared parents", but if the young ones "want to cool down", it's "a relief on a hot day."

Tuck & Roll's Drive 'Em Buggies, Flik's Fun Fair | 23 | 12 | 13

Car/Tram Ride | Duration: 4 min | Min ht: 36 | Wait: Moderate | Fastpass: No
These "gentle" "bump-or-be-bumped" "dodge 'em cars" in Flik's Fun Fair have "cute theming" with their pill-bug carapaces and Tuck and Roll's "gibberish" "comments on your or your neighbor's driving"; but while "younger children" welcome the chance "to be just a teensy bit aggressive", elders are bugged by the "ultraslow" pace.

GOLDEN STATE

Bakery Tour, The | 12 | 19 | 5

Exhibit | Duration: 10 min | Wait: None | Fastpass: No
"What's not to like" about a walk-through tour that yields a "yummy" Boudin bread sample, a "cute movie" about "making sourdough" (co-hosted by Rosie O'Donnell) and the chance to see an "automated bakery in action"? ask devotees of this San Fran transplant in Golden State; those who aren't uplifted by the vagaries of yeast call it a "one-time" stop whose "main appeal is the short line."

Grizzly River Run
27 | 28 | 27
Flume/Whitewater | Duration: 7 min | Min ht: 42 | Wait: Very Long | Fastpass: Yes
"You're gonna get wet" – even "drenched" ("beware" the "unpredictable geysers") – on this "exciting", "lavishly landscaped" "whitewater" ride in Golden State, where "inner-tube rafts" go "spiraling through caves" and "dropping down waterfalls" on a "roaring" "river trek"; "on hot days" the line "is a bear", but in winter you can sometimes "walk right in"; P.S. there are "free lockers" for stashing "valuables" or a "change of clothes."

Magic of Brother Bear, The
22 | 13 | 10
Live Show | Duration: n/a | Wait: n/a | Fastpass: No
Inspired by the 2003 flick, this "storytelling show" in Golden State is a "cute" "diversion for kids" with "energetic" ursine performers presenting an interactive ceremony that involves "summoning spirits through totem carvings"; but since the "slow-paced", "New Age" plot doesn't always "hold the interest" of tykes, it's no surprise some adults deem it unbearably "boring."

Mission Tortilla Factory
15 | 20 | 6
Exhibit | Duration: n/a | Wait: Short | Fastpass: No
For an "educational break", this "quick, entertaining tour" of a "mini-factory" in Golden State combines a "short video" about the "history of the tortilla" with an "actual working" machine turning them out; "as a bonus", *compañeros* can "munch on" a "fresh, hot" "free sample" "right off the conveyor belt"; P.S. if "you're sporting a birthday pin", you'll take away an "entire bag" of the *delicioso* "treats."

Redwood Creek Challenge Trail
26 | 17 | 16
Interactive Attraction | Duration: n/a | Min ht: 32 | Wait: None | Fastpass: No
"Take those hyper kids" to this "no-wait exercise opportunity" in Golden State and let them "burn off some energy" as they "run wild", "climb stuff" and "explore" all the "nooks and crannies" among two acres of rocks, "rope bridges", "slides and tunnels"; it's an "excellent play area" surrounded by "Yosemite" "scenery" – "and the shade is sooo nice too."

☑ Soarin' Over California
27 | 29 | 25
Simulator | Duration: 5 min | Min ht: 40 | Wait: Very Long | Fastpass: Yes
"The next best thing to hang gliding", this "visually stunning" experience "hoists riders from the ground" in front of a "massive" "Imax-type screen" that "immerses them in the illusion" they "really are soarin'" over the Golden State's "most beautiful landscapes"; whether of "orange groves, mountains" or "Disney fireworks", the "spectacular panoramic views" and "accompanying scents and sounds" are "flawlessly executed" and always "uplifting'"; P.S. "definitely" "get a Fastpass for this one."

HOLLYWOOD PICTURES BACKLOT

Animation Academy, Disney Animation
23 | 24 | 11
Interactive Attraction | Duration: 12 min | Wait: Short | Fastpass: No
"Often missed", this "underrated" Hollywood Pictures Backlot "gem" offers "easy" lessons on sketching "everyone from Mickey to

CHILD | ADULT | THRILL

Pooh" from "real Disney animators" who are "always animated themselves"; "different characters" are taught "every 30 minutes", and "best of all, you can take the drawing home" ("free souvenir!") – though the air-conditioning and "comfortable seating" seem to be major attractions as well.

"Disney's Aladdin – A Musical Spectacular" `27` `26` `17`

Live Show | Duration: 45 min | Wait: Long | Fastpass: No

"Like a Broadway production", this "lavish", "interactive" staging of the "high-flying adventures of Aladdin and Jasmine" on the Hollywood Pictures Backlot comes with "classic songs", "plenty of eye candy" "to keep the kids entranced" (including a "magic carpet soaring" over the audience) and "hilarious" "topical" "zingers" for adults courtesy of "the mugging genie"; "wowed" spectators avow it's "worth the price of park admission alone."

Hollywood Backlot Stage, The `16` `18` `10`

Live Show | Duration: n/a | Wait: n/a | Fastpass: No

"Tucked away" near the *Monsters, Inc.* ride, this large outdoor stage hosts "cute shows" dedicated to "backstage Hollywood" that fans feel "capture the essence of Disney with singing, dancing and, of course, characters"; however, a critical contingent says the erratic showtimes and lack of action make it a "waste of space" – but those shady benches are a "nice place to rest."

Monsters, Inc. Mike & Sulley to the Rescue! `26` `18` `13`

Car/Tram Ride | Duration: 3 min | Wait: Moderate | Fastpass: No

A "colorful" "retelling of the Pixar classic", this "winner" on the Hollywood Pictures Backlot is a "fun little whirl" in a "taxi through Monstropolis" on a mission "to keep Boo from the evil Randall"; thanks to "amazing" "attention to detail" – from "fabulous" animatronics to "smell-o-vision" – it's a "children's ride that won't bore adults" (particularly those who've "seen the movie"); P.S. prepare for a "surprise" ending, when "Roz says a spunky little something especially for you."

Muppet*Vision 3D `24` `21` `14`

Movie/Multimedia | Duration: 14 min | Wait: Moderate | Fastpass: No

It's a "cute" Hollywood Pictures Backlot attraction that's "starting to show its age", but this "3-D chase" flick "with some live action" still "captures" the "zany antics" of the "Muppet gang" via a "pre-show worth coming early for", "surprise special effects", "silly jokes" and a "hokey but enjoyable" storyline; expect "increasing mayhem and noise" but no "major scare factor for the little ones."

Playhouse Disney – Live on Stage! `27` `14` `15`

Live Show | Duration: 23 min | Wait: Moderate | Fastpass: No

"Wee ones" who "watch the Disney Channel" can "dance, jump" and see "their favorite characters live" amid "confetti and bubbles" at this "adorable" "interactive show" on the Hollywood Pictures Backlot; tykes get "so excited" now that a "makeover" has brought in the casts of *Handy Manny, Mickey Mouse Clubhouse, Little Einsteins* and *My Friends Tigger and Pooh*, but elders should "be forewarned: you sit on the floor."

	CHILD	ADULT	THRILL

Sorcerer's Workshop, Disney Animation
| 23 | 22 | 12 |

Interactive Attraction | Duration: 10 min | Wait: Short | Fastpass: No
This "hands-on" animation-themed "walk-through" on the Hollywood Pictures Backlot lets you "discover your inner Disney character" in the Beast's Library, do "voice-overs" for a "popular scene" from a movie in Ursula's Grotto and even "draw your own" strip; filled with stills from familiar cartoons, it's "cool" "and secretly educational" for "adults and kids alike."

Turtle Talk With Crush, Disney Animation
| 28 | 22 | 15 |

Interactive Attraction | Duration: 11 min | Wait: Moderate | Fastpass: No
Showcasing "state-of-the-art interaction", this "ingenious" show on the Hollywood Pictures Backlot presents a "live on-screen chat" with *Finding Nemo*'s "animated surfer turtle" Crush, whose "free-flowing" movements are as nimble as his "witty" "impromptu" answers to audience questions; between the "giggles" and "amazement", spectators say Pixar's "geniuses" "have outdone themselves with this one": "it so totally rocks, dude!"

☒ Twilight Zone Tower of Terror, The
| 21 | 29 | 30 |

Thrill Ride | Duration: 3 min | Min ht: 40 | Wait: Very Long | Fastpass: Yes
"It's a scream" attest admirers of this Hollywood Pictures Backlot "doozy" – the Survey's No. 1 for Thrill and Adult Appeal – where a "creepy walk-through" of the 1930s Hollywood Tower Hotel "sucks you into" the *Twilight Zone*; "items from the TV show" and a ghostly Rod Serling foreshadow a "haunted elevator" ride featuring a "white-knuckled" series of "surprise" "plummets" into "zero-G" "free fall", yielding an "intense" "rush" that all agree is "not for the faint of heart or full of stomach."

PARADISE PIER

☒ California Screamin'
| 22 | 29 | 29 |

Roller Coaster | Duration: 3 min | Min ht: 48 | Wait: Long | Fastpass: Yes
"Thrill-seekers" salute this "exquisitely designed" Paradise Pier coaster, a "real scream" in the "classic boardwalk style" that's "one of the biggest and baddest rides" around; from the "exhilarating" "55 mph launch" to the "breathtaking" "loop-de-loop" "in the shape of Mickey", it's "super-smooth", but be ready to "pull some gnarly g's"; P.S. "the single-rider line is significantly shorter."

Games of the Boardwalk
| 18 | 13 | 9 |

Arcade | Duration: n/a | Wait: n/a | Fastpass: No
"Low-tech but still a bunch of fun", these "carnival-style games" at Paradise Pier "bring you back to the old-fashioned days" as you "test your skills" with faux fishing, "knocking down clowns" and other chances to win a "stuffed toy"; but skeptics who deem them a "rip-off" advise "save your bucks and buy a souvenir instead."

Golden Zephyr
| 19 | 15 | 14 |

Spinning/Orbiting Ride | Duration: 2 min | Wait: Moderate | Fastpass: No
"Flying in circles was never so much fun" as on this Paradise Pier "swing-type ride", a "throwback" that affords "lovely" views via "chrome"-plated gondolas making a "gentle" circuit "out over the wa-

ter"; though slightly "underwhelming" (ok, some find it downright "dull"), it's a "mellow" interlude that's especially "pretty at night"; P.S. "it closes often due to wind."

Jumpin' Jellyfish

23 | 10 | 15

Other | Duration: 1 min | Min ht: 40 | Wait: Moderate | Fastpass: No
Paradise Pier's "mini-version" of the Maliboomer, this "kiddie ride" delivers "mild thrills" as it "lifts you gently" "in the tentacles of a jelly-fish" and you "float back down" as if "in a parachute"; "younger children" "love it" and grown-ups enjoy the "view from the top", though some note that height restrictions "leave a lot of small three- to four-year-olds out."

King Triton's Carousel

24 | 14 | 11

Spinning/Orbiting Ride | Duration: 2 min | Wait: Short | Fastpass: No
"It's a mad dash to get the animal of your choice" on this Paradise Pier merry-go-round, a "twist on the traditional" with its "cute array" of "brightly colored" "dolphins, seahorses, whales" and other "marine creatures"; honoring the "amusement parks that used to line California's coast", it's an "enjoyable" if "smaller" "alternative" to the King Arthur Carrousel – with a "generally shorter" wait.

Maliboomer

17 | 25 | 26

Thrill Ride | Duration: 2 min | Min ht: 52 | Wait: Moderate | Fastpass: No
"Adrenaline junkies" get their "bragging rights" from these Paradise Pier towers, which "shoot you straight up" 180 feet (like colossal versions of the sledgehammer-and-bell strength tests); the "spectacular view" up top is "worth the g-force it takes to get there", and the bouncy drop back down is "totally awesome" too; P.S. the ongoing "redo of California Adventure" will mean the end of this "carny ride."

Mulholland Madness

24 | 22 | 22

Roller Coaster | Duration: 2 min | Min ht: 42 | Wait: Long | Fastpass: Yes
"Brace yourself" for "high anxiety" aboard this "zippy li'l coaster" at Paradise Pier, a "compact" attraction that proves "scarier than it looks" once you experience the "potent jolts", "hairpin turns and steep drops" in a "bumpy" car that seems ready to "veer off the track"; though it's only a "crazy", "jerky" "carny ride", it elicits "unexpected" "screams from most."

Orange Stinger

23 | 20 | 19

Spinning/Orbiting Ride | Duration: 2 min | Min ht: 48 | Wait: Moderate | Fastpass: No
On the edge of Paradise Pier, this "buzzworthy" "variation" on an "amusement-park staple" seats "swingers" in a "flying" bee-motif chair that "twirls around in circles" ("beware, can cause dizziness") and "gently slopes up and down" within a "giant orange peel"; though "not exactly a thrill a minute", it's "faster than you'd expect" and has a "beautiful" view; N.B. the Silly Symphony Swings are set to replace it as part of the park's refurb.

S.S. rustworthy

20 | 8 | 9

Interactive Attraction | Duration: n/a | Wait: n/a | Fastpass: No
Take "a break" and "let the kids cool off" at this Paradise Pier play area themed as a fireboat run aground, where junior deckhands can "move

about the ship" and "squirt water cannons"; but mutineers cite "broken or turned-off features" and say unless you're a "tiny tot", "there has to be something better to do"; N.B. it's set to be scuttled in fall 2009 as part of the park's refurb.

Sun Wheel

21 | 22 | 21

Spinning/Orbiting Ride | Duration: 8 min 30 sec | Wait: Long | Fastpass: No
"What goes up doesn't come down for quite a while" on this 16-story Paradise Pier Ferris wheel, which lets you "choose your thrill factor" via either "tame" "stationary" gondolas that deliver little more than "a fabulous view" or the "surprisingly" "unnerving" "swinging ones" that "keep you screaming" but are "not for the queasy" (hence the "motion-sickness bags"); N.B. it's closed for retheming through spring 2009, when it will reemerge as Mickey's Fun Wheel.

⊉ Toy Story Midway Mania!

29 | 28 | 24

Car/Tram Ride | Duration: 5 min 30 sec | Wait: Very Long | Fastpass: No
Opened in mid-2008 and "an instant favorite" with "all ages", this "addictive" Paradise Pier "marriage of ride and video game" "whisks you off" wearing "3-D glasses" into "supercharged" "shooting galleries", where you wield "high-tech" "pop guns" with "virtual bullets" "to rack up scores" as "the *Toy Story* gang" "cheers you on and gives advice"; with the "adrenaline high and the laughs rolling", it's "definitely worth" the "long" waits.

CAL. ADVENTURE

Dining

GOLDEN STATE

	FOOD	DECOR	SERVICE	COST

Boudin Bread Cart *Bakery*
20 | 14 | 19 | $10

Food cart | S

Just outside Golden State's popular Bakery Tour, this cart earns plaudits for its "fresh, tasty" sourdough bread made from the 150-year-old Boudin recipe (and for a "fair" price at that); Disneyphiles favor the "adorable" loaves "shaped like Mickey Mouse", which many say make memorable "souvenirs."

Bountiful Valley Farmer's Market *Health Food*
18 | 17 | 16 | $10

Counter service | L, D, S

Variety's the name of the game at this Golden State counter appreciated for its "healthy options" (e.g. "fresh vegetables" and salads) and barbecued "chicken strips"; the "out-of-the-way" location "rarely gets foot traffic", so you may have the "plentiful" "picnic-style" seating to yourself.

Cocina Cucamonga Mexican Grill *Mexican*
15 | 16 | 15 | $17

Counter service | L, D, S

The "tortillas are fresh" (courtesy of next door's Mission Tortilla Factory) at this Golden State "cafeteria-style" cantina dishing up "large portions" of "standard" Mexican at "reasonable" prices; heat-seekers dis "bland", "Taco Bell"-ish chow, but it offers a "change" from basic "burgers-and-dogs" theme-park fare.

Farmer's Market Fruit Cart *Health Food*
20 | 15 | 17 | $8

Food cart | S

This "guilt-free" Golden State cart puts "a little Mother Nature" in your diet, offering an array of "fresh, juicy", "chilled" fruits plus nuts, "cold drinks" and "classic big dill pickles"; indulgent sorts may want to try the "chocolate-dipped strawberries."

Pacific Wharf Café *Californian*
19 | 16 | 16 | $14

Counter service | L, D, S

Take the Bakery Tour in Golden State, then spend some dough at this "antidote to greasy fare" next door; the "friendly" counter-service staff is a boon, but it's the "freshly prepared" sandwiches, "hearty" soups" served in "tasty" bread bowls and "Mickey Mouse–shaped loaves that leave guests "feeling both well fed and fed well."

Pacific Wharf Distribution Co. *American*
▽ 20 | 17 | 20 | $11

Food cart | Serves alcohol

Lagerheads longing for a "foamy delight of a malted beverage" ho over to this Golden State beer truck featuring the wares of San Dieg microbrewer Karl Strauss on tap; bonus: "great outdoor concerts" ar sometimes held in this "quiet", "secluded" area.

Rita's Baja Blenders *Mexican*
▽ 17 | 13 | 16 | $10

Food cart | Serves alcohol

For "'ritas, 'ritas and more 'ritas", park-goers flock to this old wate tower now serving as a Golden State drink stand; tipplers toas the "refreshing", "tasty" elixirs, but a few testy tequila hounds complain that the "watered-down", "pre-made" libations are "mostly sugar syrup."

Sam Andreas Shakes *Ice Cream* | 19 | 13 | 15 | $8 |

Counter service | S

Ice cream aficionados are all shook up by the "wonderful shakes" served at this earthquake-inspired Golden State counter; the "many flavors" and "choice of toppings" make this one "worth finding", but you may end up "disappointed" since "it's not always open."

Taste Pilots' Grill *American* | 17 | 18 | 15 | $15 |

Counter service | Serves alcohol | L, D, S

"Fire up your taste engines" while checking out the "declassified top-secret documents" adorning Golden State's "hangar"-like rib shack and "burger joint", serving what some deem the "park's best fast food"; while "kids go crazy for the condiment bar" (tomatoes, lettuce, etc.), parents rejoice because it "serves beer" – a "rare treat at Disney."

Vineyard Wine Bar *Californian* | 19 | 21 | 21 | $20 |

Counter service | Serves alcohol

"Grown-ups" who need to "unwind" stomp over to this "cool", "quiet" Golden State wine bar for its "fine selection" of California vintages and "inviting" patio; there's "little food available (mainly cheese)", but satisfied sippers praise the "knowledgeable staff" and warn it's "hard to get up and back to the frenzied rides."

Wine Country Trattoria *Italian* | 19 | 21 | 20 | $25 |

Table service | Reservations: Required | Serves alcohol | L, D

You may "feel like you're in Italy" thanks to this Golden State trattoria's "pleasant setting" ("a mix of Tuscany and Old California") and "tasty" Italian fare, including "wonderful" lasagna; faultfinders dis the "limited" menu, but most find compensation in the "attentive" service, "reasonable" prices and "decent" wines by the glass; P.S. patio seats afford "excellent views" of the Pixar Play Parade.

HOLLYWOOD PICTURES BACKLOT

Award Wieners *Hot Dogs* | 15 | 13 | 14 | $11 |

Counter service | L, D, S

For a "reasonably priced" fast-food fix ("by Disney standards", anyhow), frankophiles nosh on "juicy" "hot dogs with clever names", chips and cookies at this Hollywood Pictures Backlot stand; still, critics bark that the "limited menu" and occasional "slow service" can make it "not such a wiener"; N.B. regulars relish the newly expanded seating area.

Fairfax Fruit Market *Health Food* ∇ | 19 | 13 | 17 | $9 |

Food cart | S

"How can you go wrong with fruit on a hot day?" ask advocates of this self-service stand on the Hollywood Pictures Backlot; an homage to LA's famed Farmers Market, it offers apples, oranges, carrot sticks and other "quick, healthy" snacks – perfect "before the kids immerse themselves in sugar."

	FOOD	DECOR	SERVICE	COST

Schmoozies *Health Food* — ∇ 18 | 15 | 16 | $8
Counter service | S
There's "no food, just smoothies" at this counter, where sun-baked visitors converge on "hot summer days" for "refreshing" "fruit combinations and mocha-flavored" concoctions; N.B. its mod Hollywood Pictures Backlot home is based on Sunset Boulevard's iconic Crossroads of the World building.

Studio Catering Co. *American* — - | - | - | I
Counter service | S
Lights, camera, snack-tion: this shiny red truck on the Hollywood Pictures Backlot is modeled on a movie-set catering van; quick-service nibbles include grilled-chicken Caesar salads, turkey clubs, chips and drinks.

PARADISE PIER

Catch-a-Flave *Ice Cream* — ∇ 21 | 13 | 17 | $7
Counter service | L, D, S
Sweet-toothed strollers would gladly "skip lunch" to make more room for the "flavor-swirled" "soft-serve" ice cream sold at this pastel-hued Paradise Pier counter – "nothing could be better" on a hot day; P.S. hours are "irregular", so "get it when you know they're open."

Corn Dog Castle *Hot Dogs* — 19 | 12 | 16 | $10
Counter service | Food cart | L, D
"Corn dog aficionados" howl with delight over the "almost obscenely" large "links on a stick" served from this retro silver trailer on Paradise Pier; the "plump" franks coated in "crunchy, sweet cornbread" are "worth the price" (and the "calories") and "can easily be shared", though "you may not want to."

Cove Bar *American* — ∇ 18 | 20 | 19 | $21
Counter service | Serves alcohol | L, D, S
"One of the few places" to sip "top-shelf" libations inside California Adventure, this "fun hangout" in Ariel's Grotto is a place to clink glasses while "watching the sunset" over the Paradise Pier lagoon or the "faces of riders" on the California Screamin' coaster, which "zooms by" regularly; there's a limited menu of bar apps – including Buffalo wings and fried calamari – for sustenance.

Pizza Oom Mow Mow *Pizza* — 15 | 18 | 15 | $14
Counter service | L, D
It has a "fun name" and a "pure SoCal" vibe complete with "charming" "surf shack decor", but surveyors are otherwise split on this "loud, crazy" Paradise Pier counter-service eatery; fans salute "generous portions" of "surprisingly good" pizza, salad and pasta, while a few crusty skeptics find the quality "just so-so" (think "Chuck E. Cheese").

SUNSHINE PLAZA

Baker's Field Bakery *Bakery* — 17 | 17 | 16 | $10
Counter service | B, L, D, S
Maybe it's "just a place to grab a snack", but park-goers hankering for a "latte and muffin" or a "3 o'clock slump"–fighting java jolt make

tracks to this Sunshine Plaza patisserie "cleverly" modeled on a train; sandwiches, "soups in a bread bowl" and "mouthwatering" desserts ("I can taste that sticky bun now") fill out the menu.

Bur-r-r Bank Ice Cream *Ice Cream* | 20 | 17 | 17 | $9 |

Counter service | L, D, S

The aroma of "fresh waffle cones" "dipped in chocolate and sprinkles" lures sweet-seekers to this "nostalgic" Sunshine Plaza parlor inside an "old diesel locomotive" adorned with "train posters"; "generous" if "kind of pricey" scoops and "huge" sundaes ("share them with a friend") lead to "long lines", so "be prepared to wait."

CAL. ADVENTURE

Shopping

GOLDEN STATE

Fly n' Buy
20 | 20 | 20 | M

Those still flyin' after Golden State's Soarin' Over California can land at this "cool" aviation-themed garage in nearby Condor Flats; stocked with model airplanes, aviator jackets, T-shirts found "nowhere else", Soarin' souvenirs and *Cars* merch, it's a neat "place to browse", complete with an elevated race car in the middle.

P.T. Flea Market
24 | 24 | 23 | M

Because it's "soooo hard to make a choice", "knowledgeable" cast members help traders sort through the "pins and pin-related merchandise" displayed "floor to ceiling" at this small Golden State cottage just outside 'a bug's land'; even those who don't get the point will find "cute souvenirs" and "silly little goodies" for the wee ones.

Rushin' River Outfitters
24 | 24 | 23 | M

"Outdoorsy" types blaze a trail to this "cute" faux log cabin in Golden State and its hardy-yet-"upscale" pants, fleece jackets, hats and sweatshirts; it "fits right in with its surroundings" next to Grizzly River Run – and it "just so happens" water rats can conveniently pick up dry T-shirts or "even underwear" after getting "soaked on the ride."

HOLLYWOOD PICTURES BACKLOT

Gone Hollywood
25 | 24 | 24 | E

"Attentive" cast members help would-be starlets score the perfect "decorated hair scrunchy", "sparkly Mickey ears bracelet" and other glamorous goodies at this "crowded" mart near the Hollywood Pictures Backlot entrance; you'll also find *High School Musical* items, princess costumes, beads, jewelry and "lots of Hollywood memorabilia."

⊠ Off the Page
28 | 28 | 26 | E

A "fun place to look around even if you aren't buying", this Hollywood Pictures Backlot gallery is a "can't-miss for Disney fans", stocking "amazing" animation art, books and figurines (it's "the spot to go for that coveted ceramic Ursula"); "prices vary", but even devotees admit some items are "too rich for my blood."

Studio Store
∇ 24 | 24 | 23 | E

The fur flies at this "cool" Hollywood Pictures Backlot stand where *Monsters, Inc* and Muppet merchandise vie for your attention (and dollars); located near the Mike & Sulley to the Rescue! attraction, it's stocked with plush toys, games and souvenirs.

Tower Hotel Gifts
23 | 24 | 22 | M

Take the plunge at the Tower of Terror on the Hollywood Pictures the "drop in" to this "spooky" store at its exit; besides "amusing" photo of you screaming your head off, there are "cool" *Nightmare Befor Christmas* souvenirs, 'I Survived' T-shirts and "neat finds" (robes, tow els) that appear to come "right out of the Hollywood Tower Hotel."

PARADISE PIER

California Scream Cam
21 20 20 | E

Be sure to smile as you "you fly past the cameras" on the California Screamin' coaster, then stop as you exit to pick up a "wonderful souvenir" snapshot at this Paradise Pier kiosk; it has its own ups and downs, however: while service can be "engaging and prompt", some insist the photos are "too expensive."

Dinosaur Jack's Sunglass Shack
20 21 21 | M

For those "oops, I forgot my sunglasses at home, let me get a cheap pair" moments, shades-seekers can check out the "good selection" of "hats, sunglasses and sunscreen" at this Paradise Pier shop; N.B. it's beneath the giant green dino across from the Mulholland Madness coaster.

Man Hat n' Beach
▽ 24 24 23 | M

"You gotta love the name" of this "good all-around" gift shop on Paradise Pier next to Sideshow Shirts; highlights include surf-themed goods like beach hats and swimwear, plus carnival mirrors to amuse the kids.

Midway Mercantile
24 23 23 | M

After testing your virtual shooting accuracy aboard the Toy Story Midway Mania! ride on Paradise Pier, take aim at this small vendor next door; crowds make a trajectory for its "good selection" of *Toy Story*-inspired goods in "many price ranges", including T-shirts, hats, Woody dolls, towels and Mr. Potato Heads.

Point Mugu
– – – | I

Inexpensive jewelry, hair accessories and temporary tats score points at this pint-sized Paradise Pier tween scene adjacent to Man Hat n' Beach; choose from pirate, princess or Mickey themes, then show off the goods as you strut down the boardwalk.

Sideshow Shirts
– – – | M

California Adventure and other Disney-themed tanks, tees and sweatshirts take the spotlight under the faux big top across from Paradise Pier's Sun Wheel; other showstoppers include tote bags, flip-flops and seasonal gewgaws at Halloween and Christmas.

Souvenir 66
▽ 24 24 24 | M

"Reasonable" prices and a tank full of travel-themed tchotchkes put souvenir-hunters in the driver's seat at this homage to Route 66 near the Paradise Pier entrance; you can also pick up personalized Mouse ears, mugs, T-shirts, postcards and primo activity books for kids.

Treasures in Paradise
– – – | M

High School Musical must-haves draw fans of the flicks to this Paradise Pier shop across from Ariel's Grotto; other items that hit all the right notes for teens and adults include a wide selection of clothes (Paul Frank, Quiksilver, Roxy), watches and jewelry.

SUNSHINE PLAZA

Engine Ears Toys
25 26 23 | M

Mr. Potato Head is the "main attraction" at this "cute" toy depot in an oversized model train near the California Adventure entrance; the playthings – including board games, dolls and stuffed animals – "lean toward the educational", but it's the tater tots dig the most, since "you can create your own unique" spud.

Greetings From California

25 | 25 | 24 | M

This "huge", all-in-one mart on Sunshine Plaza is California Adventure's "version of Disneyland's Emporium", but with "no crowds"; Adventurers find a "little bit of everything" – from Golden State trinkets and T-shirts to personalized Mouse ears and pins – "at all price ranges", plus they can pick up any pictures taken by cast members during their visit.

DOWNTOWN DISNEY DISTRICT AND HOTELS OF THE DISNEYLAND RESORT

Downtown Disney District/Hotels

Planted just outside the parks' gates and within walking distance of all three Disneyland Resort hotels, the Downtown Disney District is an outdoor promenade with retail shops, restaurants, live music venues and a 12-theater cinema. It's busiest in the evenings, drawing post-park crowds as well as locals. Mornings are more low-key, with most shops opening at 10 AM and staying open until 10 PM Sunday through Thursday and 11 PM Friday and Saturday.

HERE'S THE PARTY: A shopper's domain during the day, Downtown Disney transforms into a dining and entertainment destination once the sun sinks. Anchored by the **House of Blues,** which often rocks past midnight with karaoke and live national acts, it offers the Resort's best variety of restaurants with full bars (Disneyland is dry, and Disney's California Adventure usually closes by 8 PM). Early-evening attractions include **Ralph Brennan's Jazz Kitchen** (daily jazz starting at 6:30 or 7 PM) as well as a mix of small bands and entertainers who perform along the promenade. And all three Disney hotels have lounges featuring bars and some form of entertainment.

REFUELING: With lunch and dinner options that include everything from a wine and tapas bar (**Uva Bar**) to **ESPN Zone,** Downtown Disney is a favorite spot to chow down for those looking for table service at (relatively) moderate prices. Keep in mind that most of the sit-down restaurants, including **Rainforest Cafe, Naples** and Ralph Brennan's Jazz Kitchen, fill up at dinnertime, so priority seating is strongly recommended (call 714-781-3463 to book a table at most Disneyland Resort restaurants). All three hotels also offer a variety of dining options, including character meals and counter service, but they're best known for special-occasion establishments like the Grand Californian's **Napa Rose** (ranked No. 1 in the Survey for Food, Decor and Service) and **Steakhouse 55** in the Disneyland Hotel.

BUY, BUY: Unlike the park retailers, Downtown Disney shops aren't centered on Mickey and friends, save for the humongous **World of Disney** (the Survey's Most Popular shop). Most stores – including **Build-a-Bear Workshop, Sephora** and **Department 56** – operate independently from the parks, but you can call **Disneyland DelivEARS** (800-362-4533) for details on all Resort shopping options.

LIGHTS, CAMERA . . .: Film buffs or the air-conditioning deprived can catch a first-run movie at the **AMC Theatres** (714-769-4AMC) near the House of Blues. Done in art deco style, it has a dozen large theaters with stadium seating and show times that run from late morning to midnight; it also hosts occasional premieres of movies such as *High School Musical 2*.

STAYING POWER: Disney operates three hotels within the Disneyland Resort, all with swimming pools, restaurants and perks for guests, including early park admission on select days. The **Grand Californian Hotel & Spa** is by far the swankiest and closest to the action (it has its own entry gate to California Adventure and some of its rooms overlook Downtown Disney), while the 14-story **Paradise Pier Hotel,** which sits across the street from the Grand Californian, appeals to families. Disney regulars favor the high-rise **Disneyland Hotel,** which anchors the west end of Downtown Disney. There are also 37 **Good Neighbor hotels** (places that maintain a level of service deemed acceptable by Disney and that can be booked through the company) within a short walk or drive of the Resort; bonuses often include discounted multiple-day park tickets and free park shuttles. (For a list, go to www.disneyland.com.)

GETTING THERE: Follow signs for Downtown Disney to get to the separate lot that abuts the shopping promenade and the Disneyland Hotel. It's free for the first three hours (or five hours with validation from a restaurant or AMC Theatres) and $6 an hour after that; there's also valet parking available in the evening. If you want to reach Downtown from within Disneyland, hop on the monorail in Tomorrowland and it will drop you off at the station right across from the **LEGO Imagination Center.** Likewise, those with prepurchased Disneyland passes can ride the monorail into the park from Downtown Disney and avoid long lines at the gates.

DOWNTOWN DISNEY

Dining

MOST POPULAR

1. Napa Rose
2. Rainforest Cafe
3. Storytellers Cafe
4. Ralph Brennan's Jazz Kitchen
5. ESPN Zone

TOP FOOD

28] Napa Rose
25] Steakhouse 55
21] Yamabuki
    Catal
20] Ralph Brennan's Jazz Kitchen

TOP FOOD (QUICK SERVICE)

21] Häagen-Dazs
20] Jamba Juice
19] Coffee House
18] Napolini
    La Brea Bakery Café

TOP DECOR RATINGS

27] Napa Rose
26] Steakhouse 55
25] Hearthstone Lounge
23] Rainforest Cafe
22] Storytellers Cafe

TOP SERVICE RATINGS

27] Napa Rose
25] Steakhouse 55
22] Yamabuki
21] Hearthstone Lounge
    Hook's Pointe

Shopping

MOST POPULAR

1. World of Disney
2. Build-a-Bear Workshop
3. Disney's Pin Traders
4. Department 56
5. LEGO Imagination Center

TOP QUALITY RATINGS

27 Marceline's Confectionery
Disney's Pin Traders
Department 56
LEGO Imagination Center
26 World of Disney

TOP DISPLAY RATINGS

27 Department 56
World of Disney
LEGO Imagination Center
Island Charters
Build-a-Bear Workshop

TOP SERVICE RATINGS

25 Build-a-Bear Workshop
24 Disney's Pin Traders
Houdini's Magic Shoppe
World of Disney
Marceline's Confectionery

DOWNTOWN DISNEY

Dining

Captain's Galley *American* ▽ 18 | 20 | 17 | $13
Disneyland Hotel | 1150 W. Magic Way
Counter service | S

Poolsiders lounging at the Disneyland Hotel's Peter Pan–themed swimming hole are hooked on this self-serve snack bar near the splash zone; expect sandwiches, sushi, salads and the requisite "french fries and drinks – and not much else."

⊠ Catal Restaurant *Mediterranean* 21 | 21 | 20 | $37
1580 S. Disneyland Dr., Ste. 103
Table service | Serves alcohol | B, L, D

Savor "flavorful", "elegantly presented" Mediterranean fare at this "romantic" haven for "fine dining" upstairs from the Uva Bar, where a "breezy" terrace affords "360-degree views" of Downtown Disney; a "classy" outpost of chef Joachim Splichal's vaunted Patina Group, it's a "quiet" "oasis" for "parents" in search of "grown-up food" and "a much-needed drink" after a day of theme-park "hustle and bustle."

Coffee House *Coffeehouse* 19 | 20 | 19 | $10
Disneyland Hotel | 1150 W. Magic Way
Counter service | B, L, D

Groggy guests perk up when they see what's brewing at the Disneyland Hotel's "tiny" red-brick cafe, a "crowded" nook for a "quick" caffeine "recharge" (cappuccino, tea, coffee elixirs); the muffins, biscotti and other baked goods have admirers too, though one wag finds them "more Costco than patisserie."

Croc's Bits 'n' Bites *American* ▽ 15 | 12 | 16 | $13
Disneyland Hotel | 1150 W. Magic Way
Counter service | L, D

"Hot-off-the-grill" chicken sandwiches, "basic burgers", nachos and the like sates guests seeking anything from a midday snack when pool-bound to a "late-night nibble" at this concession stand near the Disneyland Hotel's Sierra Tower; "simple", "fast" and "reasonable" sums it up.

Disney's PCH Grill *American* 19 | 19 | 18 | $27
Disney's Paradise Pier Hotel | 1717 S. Disneyland Dr.
Table service | Reservations: Required | Serves alcohol | B, L, D

Goofy'd-out park-goers appreciate the "relaxing atmosphere" at this "quiet" sit-down option inside the Paradise Pier Hotel; the colorful open kitchen doles out "good" if "not spectacular" fare – from "Hawaiian-tinged meals" to "made-to-order" eggs and "make-your-own" pizzas – all served by an "attentive staff"; P.S. the *Lilo & Stitch* breakfast buffet is a "blast."

ESPN Zone *American* 17 | 21 | 17 | $26
1545 S. Disneyland Dr.
Table service | Serves alcohol | L, D

"Testosterone-infused" "sports nuts" cheer this Downtown Disney chain outpost where they can watch the action on the "wall of TVs" or play "arcade and pinball games" upstairs; beyond the "good beer selection", however, many find the "pricey" bar food "unmemorable" and the service "hit or miss"; it's "noisy" too – "don't expect an intimate" meal.

Häagen-Dazs *Ice Cream* | 21 | 14 | 16 | $9
1550 S. Disneyland Dr., Ste. 103A
Counter service | S
"What's not to like" about "a cup or cone" of the "top-notch" ice cream scooped by this chain's Downtown Disney outpost; ok, it's kind of "expensive" and some question braving "long lines" for flavors "you can buy in any store", but addicts feel it's "worth it" for an HD "fix."

Hearthstone Lounge ❂ *American* | 18 | 25 | 21 | $22
Disney's Grand Californian Hotel & Spa | 1600 S. Disneyland Dr.
Table service | B, L, D, S
"Calling all grown-ups!": "sit back in cushy" Craftsman-style rockers and "unwind" by the fire in this "lovely little" "hideaway" in the Grand Californian, complete with tabletop "chess and checkers" and "excellent drinks"; it's "more bar than eating place", but the kitchen does turn out "simple, delicious" appetizers.

Hook's Pointe *Seafood* | 19 | 20 | 21 | $36
Disneyland Hotel | 1150 W. Magic Way
Table service | Serves alcohol | Reservations: Required | D
"Avast!", it's a "casual", "family-friendly" seafooder within eyeshot of the Disneyland Hotel's "cool" Never Land pool; the "entertaining" open kitchen, "quiet" atmosphere and Captain Hook–inspired decor keep landlubbers from walking the plank, though a few old salts say the "creative" fare is "hit-or-miss" – and "expensive."

House of Blues *Southern* | 16 | 21 | 17 | $34
1530 S. Disneyland Dr.
Table service | Serves alcohol | L, D
Yes, "it's a chain", but this "loud" Downtown Disney hang wins nods for its "unforgettable" "Sunday gospel brunch", live concerts and "eclectic" decor with lots of "authentic folk art"; the "dependable" "Southern comfort" grub (fried chicken, catfish nuggets) pleases most, and even detractors say you should "go for the entertainment."

Jamba Juice *Health Food* | 20 | 13 | 17 | $7
1550 S. Disneyland Dr., Ste. 102
Counter service | S
"Fruit smoothie" fanciers are juiced to have this counter-service "healthy drinks joint" in Downtown Disney, which explains the "long" if "well-organized lines"; critics froth if "you've been to one, you've been to them all" and contend it's "more expensive" than your local branch.

La Brea Bakery Café *Californian* | 18 | 14 | 16 | $17
1556 S. Disneyland Dr.
Table service | Serves alcohol | B, L, D, S
This "convenient" Downtown Disney outpost of the famed LA bakery is the "last chance" to nab a "decent latte or mocha" "before entering the parks"; highlights include "excellent bread", "delicious" breakfasts and "people-watching" from the patio, but even the "closest cold beer" to Disneyland can't stop a few faultfinders from deeming it "nothing to write home about" and "pretty darned expensive" at that.

DOWNTOWN DISNEY

	FOOD	DECOR	SERVICE	COST

Lost Bar ◗ *American* — 13 | 16 | 17 | $20
Disneyland Hotel | 1150 W. Magic Way
Table service | Serves alcohol | L, D, S

"Mellow out" over "sizable tropical drinks", "TV sports" and live music at this "lesser-known escape" in the Disneyland Hotel that's "more Captain Hook than Peter Pan"; not much effort goes into the "basic" bar food – e.g. chicken fingers, fries – but you'll enjoy hobnobbing with the "entertaining" bartenders and Mouse minions who hang here "after work."

Ⓩ Napa Rose *Californian* — 28 | 27 | 27 | $65
Disney's Grand Californian Hotel & Spa | 1600 S. Disneyland Dr.
Table service | Serves alcohol | D

You may find it "hard to believe you're at Disneyland" after sampling Andrew Sutton's "spectacular" Californian fare at this "premier" "destination" in the Grand Californian, ranked the Survey's No. 1 for Food, Decor and Service; Rose-ettes rave about the "outstanding" staff well-versed on the "phenomenal" wine list, "classy" yet "kid-friendly" atmosphere (complete with "beautiful stained-glass windows") and "innovative" menu that "changes seasonally" – "pricey", yes, but "worth every penny"; P.S. for a "special occasion", dine at the "kitchen counter" and watch the chef "work his magic."

Naples Ristorante e Pizzeria *Italian* — 18 | 18 | 18 | $30
1550 S. Disneyland Dr., Ste. 101
Table service | Serves alcohol | L, D

"Pizza freaks rejoice" over the thin-crust, "wood-fired" pies at this "casual" Patina Group trattoria on Downtown Disney's edge; *paesani* salute the "surprisingly authentic" Italian fare, "sizable" portions and patio ideal for "people-watching", outvoting the few naysayers who insist it's "nothing special", with "service that could be better for the price."

Napolini *Italian* — 18 | 16 | 17 | $17
1550 S. Disneyland Dr., Ste. 101
Counter service | L, D, S

The "take-out arm" of Downtown Disney's larger Naples restaurant, this counter-service Italian deli-pizzeria turns out pasta, panini and "genuine wood-oven" "pizza by the slice" that enthusiasts claim is "as good as" any on the East Coast; faultfinders say it's "average" at best and "on the pricey side", though still "fine if you want something fast."

Ⓩ Rainforest Cafe *American* — 12 | 23 | 14 | $25
1515 S. Disneyland Dr.
Table service | Serves alcohol | B, L, D

Diners "pay for the decor" at this Downtown Disney chain option featuring "animatronic" "jungle critters" and thunderous "lightning storms" ("enchanting" to many, but possibly "overwhelming for small children"); supporters call it a "good family place" with "reliable" American fare, but critics squawk the "novelty has worn off" and say the "obesity-huge" portions of "bland" chow are "not worth the wait or price."

Ⓩ Ralph Brennan's Jazz Kitchen *Creole* — 20 | 21 | 18 | $34
1590 S. Disneyland Dr.
Table service | Serves alcohol | L, D

"Classic live jazz" and "rich" Creole cooking make this Downtown Disney version of the New Orleans icon "as close to Louisiana as you can get" in these parts; purists say it's "nowhere near the real Brennan's", but it's an "escape from Planet Disney", and to also escape the "loud" dining room, "sit on the balcony" and enjoy an "unfettered" fireworks view along with the likes of "out-of-this-world bananas Foster."

Z Steakhouse 55 *Steak*   25 | 26 | 25 | $52
Disneyland Hotel | 1150 W. Magic Way
Table service | Serves alcohol | B, L, D
As if the "fantastic steaks" and "impressive wine list" weren't enough, this "elegant" "adult gem" at the Disneyland Hotel captures the spirit of "old Hollywood", with "cushy banquettes" and "vintage" "black-and-white" photographs of "1950s movie stars"; the "prompt, courteous" staff delivers "impeccable service" too – just "don't forget your wallet."

Z Storytellers Cafe *Californian*   20 | 22 | 21 | $30
Disney's Grand Californian Hotel & Spa | 1600 S. Disneyland Dr.
Table service | Reservations: Required | Serves alcohol | B, L, D
Even "jaded Disneyphiles" tell fond stories about this "family-friendly" Grand Californian "favorite", a "cozy" retreat from the parks' "hustle and bustle" featuring "hand-carved wooden panels" and "roaring" fireplaces; the Californian fare (including "to-die-for" corn chowder) can be ordered "off the menu" or sampled from the "top-notch buffet", and while it's "not inexpensive", most deem it "worth the price"; P.S. the "wonderful" Chip & Dale character breakfast invades the space daily.

Surfside Lounge *American*   - | - | - | M
Disney's Paradise Pier Hotel | 1717 S. Disneyland Dr.
Table service | Serves alcohol | L, D
Guests at the Paradise Pier Hotel drop anchor at this nautical-themed lobby lounge to check e-mail via free WiFi or to power up for the parks with specialty-coffee drinks, breakfast and lunch (burgers, grilled chicken sandwich, salads); at night, a full bar turns it into a hub for cocktails and conversation.

Tortilla Jo's *Mexican*   14 | 14 | 13 | $27
1510 S. Disneyland Dr.
Table service | Serves alcohol | L, D
A "wonderful selection" of 100-plus tequilas adds zing to the "good margaritas" at this Patina Group Mexican, a "spacious" Downtown Disney cantina that "fills up quickly" when the parks empty; while some insist it's "just the thing" for a "recharge", others are "not at all impressed", citing occasional "slow" service and "bland grub" ("I've had better food from a taco truck").

Tortilla Jo's Taqueria *Mexican*   17 | 16 | 17 | $17
1510 S. Disneyland Dr.
Counter service | L, D, S
"For a fraction of what they charge" at its bigger Patina Group sibling, this Downtown Disney "take-out window" offers "pretty good" Mexican fare and "outside seating"; if "you're on the go", vets recommend toting a "Mexicone", fried tortillas "shaped like ice cream cones and stuffed with taco ingredients."

DOWNTOWN DISNEY

Uva Bar *Mediterranean*   16 | 18 | 17 | $26
1580 S. Disneyland Dr., Ste. 103
Table service | Serves alcohol | L, D, S
"People-watch and imbibe" at this "casual" "patio bar" "smack dab in
the middle of Downtown Disney", a "less expensive" alternative to upstairs sib Catal and a place "for adults to pause and relax" over a
"snack and a pick-me-up"; its "tasty" Med-style tapas and "decent
wine list" are "therapeutic", and the surrounding "action" could even
"be called a scene."

Wetzel's Pretzels *Pretzels*   17 | 11 | 14 | $8
1540 S. Disneyland Dr., Ste. 103
Counter service | L, D, S
"You know what you're getting" at this Downtown Disney kiosk where
the popular chain's "hot, fresh pretzels" and "pretzel dogs" are doled
out with "refreshing lemonade" ("now that's a meal"); one unhappy
twist: a few gripe that service "leaves something to be desired."

White Water Snacks *American*   17 | 15 | 17 | $13
Disney's Grand Californian Hotel & Spa | 1600 S. Disneyland Dr.
Counter service | L, D, S
Considered one of the Resort's "best secrets" by fans, this "seldom
busy", "cafeteria-style" "refuge" with a campground vibe and "lots of
indoor seating" is "hidden away" near the Grand Californian pool;
even if the "basic" American menu (burgers, sandwiches, "some
healthy choices") doesn't satisfy everyone, the prices usually do: you
won't go "overboard on your budget."

Wine Cellar *American*   ▽ 19 | 22 | 22 | $24
Disneyland Hotel | 1150 W. Magic Way
Table service | Serves alcohol | D
"Avoid the tourist crowds" at this "intimate" "little" wine bar, a "hidden treasure" below Hook's Pointe restaurant in the Disneyland Hotel;
enthused oenophiles uncork praise for the "friendly", "knowledgeable"
cast members and "nice selection" of California vino, complemented
by free "cheese and crackers."

Ⓩ Yamabuki *Japanese*   21 | 21 | 22 | $42
Disney's Paradise Pier Hotel | 1717 S. Disneyland Dr.
Table service | Reservations: Required | Serves alcohol | L, D
Disney's "usual attention to detail" reveals itself in the "beautiful ambiance" and "consistent" cuisine at this "surprising" Japanese in the
Paradise Pier Hotel; from the "fresh", "delicious" sushi and "cook-it-
yourself shabu-shabu" to the sake selection, park-goers are in for
"something different" – especially if they "sit traditionally on the floor"
"for a more interesting experience."

Hotels

Ratings & Symbols

Rooms, Service, Dining and **Facilities** are rated on the Zagat 0 to 30 scale.

✚ children's programs   Ⓢ notable spa facilities
♨ views

Disneyland Hotel, The ✚ | 16 | 21 | 17 | 21 | $275 |

1150 W. Magic Way | 714-778-6600 | 908 rooms, 61 suites
The Resort's "original on-site hotel" is "geared for the entire family" with its "Disney-decorated rooms", "wonderful" "Peter Pan–themed pool" and "convenient" location adjacent to Downtown (complete with a nearby "monorail stop"); maybe it's "not the swankiest" and the "outdated" facilities "could use an upgrade" (especially "for the rates they charge"), but "accommodating" staffers help compensate; N.B. the resident Steakhouse 55 is named for the year Disneyland opened.

Disney's Grand Californian | 22 | 24 | 23 | 25 | $519 |
Hotel & Spa ✚♨Ⓢ

1600 S. Disneyland Dr. | 714-635-2300 | 701 rooms, 44 suites
"Grand" indeed describes this "splurge" next to California Adventure, where "unforgettable visits" are enhanced by "outstanding" service, "superb" dining (it's home to Napa Rose, the Survey's No. 1 for Food, Decor and Service) and such niceties as a "stunning" "Craftsman-style" lobby with "giant fireplace", a waterslide-equipped pool and the Mandara Spa; many rooms boast "fabulous views", and even if some feel they "could be bigger" given the "big-bucks" bills, most find it all "well worth it"; N.B. an ongoing expansion will add about 250 rooms by the end of 2009.

Disney's Paradise Pier Hotel ✚♨ | 16 | 21 | 16 | 18 | $265 |

1717 S. Disneyland Dr. | 714-999-0990 | 469 rooms, 20 suites
Comprising two "beach-themed" towers, the smallest of the Resort's hotels may be a "bit of a walk" from the parks, but it provides "quite comfortable" rooms, "professional" service and a rooftop pool with a "cool" "waterslide for the kids" (inspired by a wooden roller coaster); however, guests who grouse about its "generic" ambiance and "limited dining" "wish there were more" on offer besides "nice prices."

DOWNTOWN DISNEY

HOTELS

Shopping

Amazing Pictures
25 | **23** | **23** | **E**

1580 S. Disneyland Dr., Ste. 206

Cast members put you in the picture at this outdoor kiosk near the Downtown Disney monorail station; after selecting which body you want from a large display, get your headshot taken and watch as it's superimposed upon the shoulders of athletes, superheroes and movie stars.

Anne Geddes
24 | **24** | **22** | **VE**

1570 S. Disneyland Dr., Ste. 105

Fans of photographer Anne Geddes "love" her "darling" if "expensive" infant and children's clothes, plus the "oversized portraits that make you go wow" at this "well-done" Downtown Disney store; still, a few skeptics gripe that "cute only goes so far" and find the "realistic-looking" dolls "kinda creepy"; N.B. a play area keeps kids busy while parents browse.

Basin
25 | **24** | **22** | **M**

1550 S. Disneyland Dr., Ste. 102

Bubble buffs sniff out this "inviting", "divine-smelling" Downtown Disney shop featuring "good-quality" bath products and service that "makes you feel right at home"; the "wonderfully decorated", "hand-made" soaps and bath bombs make "nice presents for teenage girls" and, better yet, help mom unwind "in the hotel bathtub."

☒ Build-a-Bear Workshop
26 | **27** | **25** | **M**

1540 S. Disneyland Dr., Ste. 101

Kids adore this "too cute" Downtown Disney store, where "friendly" staffers help them "choose a bear, stuff it, dress it and name it" ("how cool is that?"); while fans roar with approval over the "good-quality", "moderately priced" ursines and the "exclusive" Disney plush, some bad news bearers growl about "long lines" and say the "accessories can add up" – so "you may end up paying a lot for a stuffed animal in a dress."

Compass Books
25 | **24** | **23** | **M**

1565 S. Disneyland Dr., Ste. 102

A "must stop" for bibliophiles, this "quaint little" Downtown Disney bookstore/cafe near the Disneyland Hotel carries a "wide variety" of volumes "for all ages" – including Mouse-related reads; tome-keepers commend the organized displays and "handpicked-selection feel", while caffeine addicts gush over the "great coffee" and long hours ("it stays open late and opens early").

Department 56
27 | **27** | **22** | **E**

1540 S. Disneyland Dr., Ste. 102

Even Scrooge McDuck would admire the "amazing" Christmas and Halloween displays at this "goes-all-out" Downtown Disney depot stocking all manner of "holiday kitsch"; "no matter what you collect", it's a "neat" place to browse, and it's "a must for miniature Christmas village" aficionados, though grinches warn "be prepared to break the bank."

Disney's Pin Traders
27 | 25 | 24 | M

1560 S. Disneyland Dr.

You'll find "every pin known to Mouse-kind" at this "collector's paradise" next to the Downtown Disney monorail station; yes, purchases can "add up once you get to the register", but die-hard "pinners" "are hooked" on the "easy one-stop shopping" and the chance to connect with other traders.

Disney Vault 28
24 | 24 | 21 | VE

1580 S. Disneyland Dr., Ste. 104

"Think hip, not dorky" when entering this "trendy, upscale" Downtown Disney boutique featuring "fabulous" Tarina Tarantino jewelry, Betsey Johnson bags and "fun clothes" displayed amid elaborate chandeliers and etched mirrors; but detractors find it all "kinda scary", complaining that's it "too crowded" and "too expensive" ("bring your life savings with you").

Fossil
26 | 25 | 23 | E

1580 S. Disneyland Dr., Ste. 103

Admirers make no bones about the "cool", "elegant" selection of leather wallets, belts, watches and "exceptional bags" at this "small" Downtown Disney chain link; gift-givers appreciate its wide range of styles for guys as well as gals ("I give all the men in my life gifts from here every year").

Houdini's Magic Shoppe
23 | 24 | 24 | M

1580 S. Disneyland Dr., Ste. 206

It's no illusion: sorcerers' apprentices relish this "cute", "crowded" kiosk near World of Disney that's chock-full of "old-fashioned, inexpensive" magic tricks and "more sophisticated props"; while there are "entertaining" demos, some yearn for a "better selection" and warn that the enchantment-challenged may pick up items here, then "forget how to work them."

Illuminations
26 | 26 | 22 | M

1580 S. Disneyland Dr., Ste. 102

Exploring this "good-smelling" Downtown Disney retailer makes scents for candle lovers who bestow glowing praise on its "excellent selection" of "beautiful", "original-looking" offerings; then again, a handful of naysayers wax indignant that the "often dark", "cluttered" store is "straight out of your local mall" – and with higher prices.

Island Charters
25 | 27 | 21 | E

1580 S. Disneyland Dr., Ste. 101

Aviation meets "Aloha shirts" at this "relaxed" Downtown Disney hangar where you'll find everything from "lots of Tommy Bahama" duds to hand-carved aircraft models – "just be prepared to chart a course for the poor house if you buy too much"; N.B. consider a stopover to ogle the model airplanes hanging from the ceiling.

Kaman's Art Shoppe
- | - | - | M

1580 S. Disneyland Dr., Ste. 206

Face-painting artists transform kids and adults alike into peacocks, clowns and lions at this Downtown Disney kiosk (a washcloth does the

DOWNTOWN DISNEY

trick when it's time to remove); you can also have your name drawn in fancy lettering, then framed while you wait; N.B. look for other locations in Fantasyland in Disneyland (where it's known as Fairytale Arts) and on California Adventure's Paradise Pier.

LEGO Imagination Center
27 | 27 | 21 | M

1585 S. Disneyland Dr.

"LEGOmaniacs" "think they've died and gone to heaven" at this "giant" Downtown Disney store; while the brickarati browse the "fantastic" collection of the "latest sets and hard-to-find items" and play in the "hands-on building section", others gawk at the "elaborate" LEGO sculptures ("works of art themselves"); tip: "ask about the frequent buyers' program", as things can get "pricey."

Marceline's Confectionery
27 | 26 | 24 | M

1580 S. Disneyland Dr., Ste. 104

"A dentist's dream and dieter's doom", this "old-fashioned" sweet shop in Downtown Disney "hits the spot" with its "scrumptious" handmade confections – regulars single out the "Mickey Mouse Rice Krispies treats", caramel apples and chocolate-dipped marshmallows; if the lines are too long, it's still a treat just to "watch the candy preparation" through the window.

Pearl Factory
∇ 23 | 21 | 24 | E

1580 S. Disneyland Dr., Ste. 206

Little ones enjoy "choosing their own oyster" and having a necklace or charm made with the pearl inside at this Downtown Disney kiosk near the monorail station; the 'rents, however, may be a little shell-shocked at the tab.

Quiksilver
24 | 23 | 20 | E

1570 S. Disneyland Dr., Ste. 103

"So SoCal", this shop near the Grand Californian Hotel & Spa caters to the surf and skateboard crowd with its "up-to-date" selection of "expensive but good" board shorts, shirts, caps and accessories – i.e. the "ultimate California dream" duds; still, a few landlubbers gripe that, given the store's location, it "should incorporate Mickey Mouse into some of the designs."

Sephora
26 | 24 | 22 | E

1570 S. Disneyland Dr., Ste. 101

Yes, "you can stay pretty in Wonderland" thanks to this Downtown Disney outpost of the national beauty-products chain, offering a "girlie break from the rides" via its "treasure trove" of "glamorous" goods; while fans adore its "knowledgeable" staff and "generous samples", a few critics would rather take a powder and just "go to the mall."

Something Silver
∇ 27 | 26 | 25 | E

1580 S. Disneyland Dr., Ste. 105

There's "always something different and sparkling" in this "elegant" "gift destination" next to Downtown Disney's Catal Restaurant; it's a "must-see" for its array of "unique" silver jewelry, and even if you're not in the market for a major piece, devotees recommend browsing its lode of key chains, money clips and charms.

	QUALITY	DISPLAY	SERVICE	COST

Sunglass Icon
▽ 26 | 21 | 23 | E

1570 S. Disneyland Dr., Ste. 104
Duck into this sleek store just west of World of Disney for a wide selection of designer shades (Oakley, AX, Gucci, Guess) in a variety of styles and prices; N.B. a cart across from La Brea Bakery near the tram drop-off offers a smaller but similar choice of eyewear and opens daily at 8:30 AM.

Tom Kelly Caricatures
▽ 28 | 25 | 26 | E

1580 S. Disneyland Dr., Ste. 206
Park-goers drawn to this "cute" kiosk near the LEGO Imagination Center literally become part of the picture in Downtown Disney – just sit and smile as Orange County artist Tom Kelly and his "friendly staff" sketch you and your pals in various backdrops and costumes.

☒ World of Disney
26 | 27 | 24 | M

1560 S. Disneyland Dr.
The "mecca of all Disney shopping", this "block-long" Downtown Disney colossus – voted the Survey's Most Popular store – stocks a "fantastic array" of Mouseke-wares "for every budget", from plush toys to fine china and apparel; while some warn it's "almost overwhelming" and can be "super crowded" (you may lose family members, "whether you want to or not"), most agree it's a Mickey lover's "paradise."

CHARACTER DINING

Character Dining

Character meals guarantee the kids face time with the likes of Goofy, Ariel and other animated Disney stars who make a point of stopping by each table for hugs and photo ops. Food is usually served buffet-style (though à la carte options are also available) with the cost averaging about $25–$35 for adults and $13–$15 for ages three–nine (tip not included).

THE OPTIONS: The **Minnie & Friends** breakfast at the Plaza Inn is the only character meal you'll find in Disneyland itself, while over in Disney's California Adventure, **Ariel's Grotto** supplies a rotating slate of princesses and serves breakfast, lunch and dinner. Each hotel offers character dining – **Goofy's Kitchen,** known for its peanut-butter-and-jelly pizza and all-day hours at the Disneyland Hotel, is a favorite, while the **Lilo & Stitch Aloha Breakfast** at the Paradise Pier Hotel's PCH Grill features a Hawaiian theme complete with flower leis for guests. The Grand Californian's Storytellers Cafe showcases lesser-known characters like Terk from *Tarzan* at the **Chip 'n Dale Critter** breakfast.

BOOK IT: You can reserve priority seating for character dining up to 60 days in advance by calling 714-781-3463, though walk-up seating is often available on weekdays.

Character Dining

Ariel's Disney Princess Celebration *American* | 17 | 21 | 24 | 17 |

Disney's California Adventure Park, Paradise Pier | Ariel's Grotto

"A thrill" for "little girls", this "fun" dining experience at Ariel's Grotto on California Adventure's Paradise Pier provides the "royal princess treatment" as "Ariel herself" and her noble peers "visit your table" for a "one-on-one experience" complete with autographs and "photo time"; the three-course American "set menu" (lunch and dinner only) is "rather pricey" and "fairly forgettable", but "let's face it, no one is there for the food."

Chip 'n Dale Critter Breakfast *American* | 23 | 23 | 22 | 20 |

Disney's Grand Californian Hotel & Spa | Storytellers Cafe | 1600 S. Disneyland Dr.

For "a great way to start the day", scamper to this all-you-can-eat breakfast buffet (including "Mickey waffles") in the "woodsy" Grand Californian's Storytellers Cafe, featuring "plenty of characters" to "hug and take pictures with" as you "fill up" on a "wide selection" of "good food"; the "excellent" staff also serves an à la carte menu, and it's "worth every penny" just "to see happy kids" (parents are "pretty jazzed too").

Goofy's Kitchen *American* | 22 | 23 | 25 | 21 |

Disneyland Hotel | 1150 W. Magic Way

"You're never too old" for this "very interactive" family "favorite" in the Disneyland Hotel, an unlimited "buffet-style" American spread with a "vast supply of kid-friendly foods" as well as "tasty" grown-up grub; overseen by chef Goofy and an "extensive" cast of characters who periodically gather for "rousing" "drumming and dancing", it's such "a blast" that few fret if it's "a little expensive"; P.S. insiders "suggest going for breakfast", though it also serves lunch and dinner.

Lilo & Stitch Aloha Breakfast *American* | 21 | 23 | 23 | 20 |

Disney's Paradise Pier Hotel | Disney's PCH Grill | 1717 S. Disneyland Dr.

"Learn the hula with Lilo and Stitch" at the Paradise Pier Hotel's "cool" breakfast luau, a "yummy" all-you-can-eat buffet that pays tribute to the movie with its "enjoyable" "Hawaiian atmosphere"; "well-run" by a "super-friendly staff", it allows for "abundant character time" since there's "less of a crowd" here than at the other morning meet-ups.

Minnie & Friends – Breakfast in the Park *American* | 22 | 23 | 24 | 21 |

Disneyland Park, Main Street, U.S.A. | Plaza Inn

With its "extensive" buffet and "large showing" of "familiar characters", this "fabulous" breakfast in Main Street's Plaza Inn is sure to "stuff and entertain you"; Minnie and her minions "come to your table nonstop" to "pose for pictures and sign autograph books", ensuring you "walk out with many memories" – and if you "go early", already "being inside the park is a major plus."

CHAR. DINING

INDEXES

Locations are indicated by the following abbreviations: Disneyland Park=DP;
Disney's California Adventure=DCA; and Downtown Disney District=DD.

disneyland.com | 714-781-4565   85

Attractions Types

Includes attraction names and locations.

ANIMATRONIC SHOW

Enchanted Tiki Room |
   DP, Adventureland

BOAT RIDE

Davy Crockett's Canoes |
   DP, Critter Country

Finding Nemo Sub Voyage |
   DP, Tomorrowland

"it's a small world" | DP, Fantasyland

Jungle Cruise | DP, Adventureland

Mark Twain Boat | DP, Frontierland

Z Pirates of Caribbean |
   DP, New Orleans Sq.

Sailing Ship Columbia |
   DP, Frontierland

Storybook Land Boats |
   DP, Fantasyland

CAR/TRAM RIDE

Alice in Wonderland |
   DP, Fantasyland

Autopia | DP, Tomorrowland

Z Buzz Lightyear Astro Blast |
   DP, Tomorrowland

Fire Engine, Main St. Vehicles |
   DP, Main St.

Haunted Mansion |
   DP, New Orleans Sq.

Horse-Drawn Street Cars |
   DP, Main St.

Horseless Carriage | DP, Main St.

Z Indiana Jones Adventure |
   DP, Adventureland

Many Adventures of Pooh |
   DP, Critter Country

Monsters, Inc. Mike & Sulley |
   DCA, Hollywood Pictures

Mr. Toad's Wild Ride |
   DP, Fantasyland

Omnibus | DP, Main St.

Peter Pan's Flight | DP, Fantasyland

Pinocchio's Journey |
   DP, Fantasyland

Roger Rabbit's Spin | DP, Toontown

Snow White's Adventures |
   DP, Fantasyland

Z Toy Story Midway Mania! |
   DCA, Paradise Pier

Tuck & Roll's Buggies |
   DCA, "a bug's land"

EXHIBIT

Bakery Tour | DCA, Golden State

Innoventions | DP, Tomorrowland

Mission Tortilla Factory |
   DCA, Golden State

FLUME/ WHITEWATER

Grizzly River Run |
   DCA, Golden State

Z Splash Mountain |
   DP, Critter Country

INTERACTIVE ATTRACTION

Animation Academy |
   DCA, Hollywood Pictures

Big Thunder Ranch |
   DP, Frontierland

Bountiful Valley Farm |
   DCA, "a bug's land"

Chip 'n Dale Tree | DP, Toontown

Disney Princess Faire |
   DP, Fantasyland

Donald's Boat | DP, Toontown

Goofy's Playhouse | DP, Toontown

Meet Pooh & Friends |
   DP, Critter Country

Mickey's House | DP, Toontown

Minnie's House | DP, Toontown

Pirate's Lair | DP, Frontierland

Pixie Hollow | DP, Fantasyland

Princess Dot Puddle Park |
   DCA, "a bug's land"

Redwood Creek Trail |
   DCA, Golden State

Sorcerer's Workshop |
   DCA, Hollywood Pictures

S.S. rustworthy |
   DCA, Paradise Pier

Tarzan's Treehouse |
   DP, Adventureland

Turtle Talk With Crush |
   DCA, Hollywood Pictures

LIVE SHOW

"Disney's Aladdin" |
   DCA, Hollywood Pictures

Disney's Electrical Parade | DCA

Fantasmic! | DP, Frontierland

Golden Horseshoe | DP, Frontierland

High School Musical 3 | DCA

Hollywood Backlot Stage |
   DCA, Hollywood Pictures

Jedi Training | DP, Tomorrowland

Magic of Brother Bear |
   DCA, Golden State

Pixar Play Parade | DCA

Playhouse Disney Live |
   DCA, Hollywood Pictures

Sword in Stone | DP, Fantasyland

Walt Disney's Parade of Dreams | DP

MOVIE/MULTIMEDIA

Disneyland: First 50 Years |
   DP, Main St.

"Honey, I Shrunk the Audience" |
   DP, Tomorrowland

It's Tough to Be a Bug! |
   DCA, "a bug's land"

Main St. Cinema | DP, Main St.

Muppet*Vision 3D |
   DCA, Hollywood Pictures

OTHER TYPES OF ATTRACTIONS

Frontierland Shootin' | Arcade |
   DP, Frontierland

Games of Boardwalk | Arcade |
   DCA, Paradise Pier

Jumpin' Jellyfish | Parachute |
   DCA, Paradise Pier

⚡ "Remember/Dreams Come
   True" | Fireworks | DP

Starcade | Arcade | DP, Tomorrowland

ROLLER COASTER/THRILL RIDE

Big Thunder Mtn. Rail |
   DP, Frontierland

⚡ California Screamin' |
   DCA, Paradise Pier

Gadget's Go Coaster | DP, Toontown

⚡ Indiana Jones Adventure |
   DP, Adventureland

Maliboomer | DCA, Paradise Pier

Matterhorn Bobsleds |
   DP, Fantasyland

Mulholland Madness |
   DCA, Paradise Pier

⚡ Space Mountain |
   DP, Tomorrowland

⚡ Twilight Zone Tower |
   DCA, Hollywood Pictures

SIMULATOR

⚡ Soarin' Over California |
   DCA, Golden State

Star Tours | DP, Tomorrowland

SPINNING/ORBITING RIDE

Astro Orbitor | DP, Tomorrowland

Dumbo/Flying Elephant |
   DP, Fantasyland

Flik's Flyers | DCA, "a bug's land"

Francis' Ladybug | DCA, "a bug's land"

Golden Zephyr | DCA, Paradise Pier

King Arthur Carrousel | DP, Fantasyland

King Triton's Carousel |
  DCA, Paradise Pier
Mad Tea Party | **DP, Fantasyland**
Orange Stinger | **DCA, Paradise Pier**
Sun Wheel | **DCA, Paradise Pier**

TOUR
Cruzin' Cal. Adventure Tour | **DCA**
Discover the Magic Tour | **DP**
Holiday Time Tour | **DP**
Sleeping Beauty Castle |
  DP, Fantasyland

VIP Tour | **DP**
Walk in Walt's Footsteps | **DP**
Welcome to Disneyland Tour | **DP**

TRAIN
Casey Jr. Circus Train |
  DP, Fantasyland
Disneyland Monorail |
  DP, Tomorrowland
Disneyland Railroad | **DP, Main St.**
Heimlich's Train | **DCA, "a bug's land"**

Attractions Special Features

Includes attraction names and locations.

EDUCATIONAL

Animation Academy |
DCA, Hollywood Pictures

Bountiful Valley Farm |
DCA, "a bug's land"

Disneyland: First 50 Years |
DP, Main St.

Innovations | **DP, Tomorrowland**

Sorcerer's Workshop |
DCA, Hollywood Pictures

GUIDED TOURS

Cruzin' Cal. Adventure Tour | **DCA**

Discover the Magic Tour | **DP**

Holiday Time Tour | **DP**

VIP Tour | **DP**

Walk in Walt's Footsteps | **DP**

Welcome to Disneyland Tour | **DP**

MUST-SEES

☑ California Screamin' |
DCA, Paradise Pier

Disney's Electrical Parade | **DCA**

Fantasmic! | **DP, Frontierland**

☑ Indiana Jones Adventure |
DP, Adventureland

"it's a small world" |
DP, Fantasyland

Matterhorn Bobsleds |
DP, Fantasyland

☑ Pirates of Caribbean |
DP, New Orleans Sq.

"Remember/Dreams Come True" |
DP

Soarin' Over California |
DCA, Golden State

Space Mountain |
DP, Tomorrowland

Splash Mountain |
DP, Critter Country

☑ Toy Story Midway Mania! |
DCA, Paradise Pier

☑ Twilight Zone Tower |
DCA, Hollywood Pictures

RAINY DAY APPROPRIATE

Animation Academy |
DCA, Hollywood Pictures

Disneyland Railroad | **DP, Main St.**

"Disney's Aladdin" |
DCA, Hollywood Pictures

Enchanted Tiki Room |
DP, Adventureland

Finding Nemo Sub Voyage |
DP, Tomorrowland

Frontierland Shootin' | **DP, Frontierland**

Golden Horseshoe | **DP, Frontierland**

"Honey, I Shrunk the Audience" |
DP, Tomorrowland

Innoventions | **DP, Tomorrowland**

"it's a small world" | **DP, Fantasyland**

It's Tough to Be a Bug! |
DCA, "a bug's land"

Main St. Cinema | **DP, Main St.**

Muppet*Vision 3D |
DCA, Hollywood Pictures

Playhouse Disney Live |
DCA, Hollywood Pictures

☑ Soarin' Over California |
DCA, Golden State

Sorcerer's Workshop |
DCA, Hollywood Pictures

Turtle Talk With Crush |
DCA, Hollywood Pictures

TEENS TOO

(13 & Above)

Autopia | **DP, Tomorrowland**

Big Thunder Mtn. Rail |
DP, Frontierland

Z Buzz Lightyear Astro Blast |
   DP, Tomorrowland
Z California Screamin' |
   DCA, Paradise Pier
"Disney's Aladdin" |
   DCA, Hollywood Pictures
Haunted Mansion |
   DP, New Orleans Sq.
High School Musical 3 | DCA
Z Indiana Jones Adventure |
   DP, Adventureland
Jedi Training | DP, Tomorrowland
Mulholland Madness |
   DCA, Paradise Pier
Sleeping Beauty Castle |
   DP, Fantasyland
Z Space Mountain |
   DP, Tomorrowland
Z Splash Mountain |
   DP, Critter Country
Starcade | DP, Tomorrowland
Star Tours | DP, Tomorrowland
Z Toy Story Midway Mania! |
   DCA, Paradise Pier
Z Twilight Zone Tower |
   DCA, Hollywood Pictures

TODDLERS
(3 & Under)
Casey Jr. Circus Train |
   DP, Fantasyland
Chip 'n Dale Tree | DP, Toontown
Heimlich's Train | DCA, "a bug's land"
King Arthur Carrousel |
   DP, Fantasyland
King Triton's Carousel |
   DCA, Paradise Pier
Many Adventures of Pooh |
   DP, Critter Country
Meet Pooh & Friends |
   DP, Critter Country
Mickey's House | DP, Toontown
Minnie's House | DP, Toontown

Playhouse Disney Live |
   DCA, Hollywood Pictures
Princess Dot Puddle Park |
   DCA, "a bug's land"
Sleeping Beauty Castle |
   DP, Fantasyland

YOUNG CHILDREN
(4-7)
Alice in Wonderland | DP, Fantasyland
Big Thunder Ranch | DP, Frontierland
Z Buzz Lightyear Astro Blast |
   DP, Tomorrowland
Casey Jr. Circus Train |
   DP, Fantasyland
Chip 'n Dale Tree | DP, Toontown
Disney Princess Faire |
   DP, Fantasyland
Donald's Boat | DP, Toontown
Dumbo/Flying Elephant |
   DP, Fantasyland
Finding Nemo Sub Voyage |
   DP, Tomorrowland
Flik's Flyers | DCA, "a bug's land"
Francis' Ladybug | DCA, "a bug's land"
Gadget's Go Coaster | DP, Toontown
Goofy's Playhouse | DP, Toontown
Heimlich's Train | DCA, "a bug's land"
"it's a small world" | DP, Fantasyland
It's Tough to Be a Bug! |
   DCA, "a bug's land"
Jedi Training | DP, Tomorrowland
Jumpin' Jellyfish | DCA, Paradise Pier
King Arthur Carrousel |
   DP, Fantasyland
King Triton's Carousel |
   DCA, Paradise Pier
Magic of Brother Bear |
   DCA, Golden State
Many Adventures of Pooh |
   DP, Critter Country
Meet Pooh & Friends |
   DP, Critter Country

ATTRACTIONS

SPECIAL FFEATURES

Dining Cuisines

Includes restaurant names and locations.

AMERICAN (TRADITIONAL)

Award Wieners |
  DCA, Hollywood Pictures

Bengal BBQ | **DP, Adventureland**

Captain's Galley |
  DD, Disneyland Hotel

Carnation Café | **DP, Main St.**

Clarabelle's | **DP, Toontown**

Coffee House |
  DD, Disneyland Hotel

Cove Bar | **DCA, Paradise Pier**

Croc's Bits 'n' Bites |
  DD, Disneyland Hotel

Daisy's Diner | **DP, Toontown**

Disney's PCH Grill |
  DD, Paradise Pier Hotel

Enchanted Cottage |
  DP, Fantasyland

ESPN Zone | **DD**

Golden Horseshoe |
  DP, Frontierland

Hearthstone |
  DD, Grand Californian Hotel

Hook's Pointe |
  DD, Disneyland Hotel

Hungry Bear | **DP, Critter Country**

Lost Bar | **DD, Disneyland Hotel**

Mint Julep | **DP, New Orleans Sq.**

Pacific Wharf Dist. |
  DCA, Golden State

Plaza Inn | **DP, Main St.**

Pluto's Dog Hse. | **DP, Toontown**

☑ Rainforest Cafe | **DD**

Rancho/Zocalo | **DP, Frontierland**

Refreshment Corner | **DP, Main St.**

River Belle Terr. | **DP, Frontierland**

Stage Door Café | **DP, Frontierland**

Studio Catering Co. |
  DCA, Hollywood Pictures

Surfside Lounge |
  DD, Paradise Pier Hotel

Taste Pilots' | **DCA, Golden State**

Tomorrowland Terr. |
  DP, Tomorrowland

Toon Up Treats | **DP, Toontown**

Village Haus | **DP, Fantasyland**

White Water |
  DD, Grand Californian Hotel

Wine Cellar | **DD, Disneyland Hotel**

BAKERIES

Baker's Field | **DCA, Sunshine Plaza**

Blue Ribbon Bakery | **DP, Main St.**

Boudin Bread | **DCA, Golden State**

La Brea | **DD**

CAJUN

☑ Blue Bayou | **DP, New Orleans Sq.**

Café Orleans | **DP, New Orleans Sq.**

French Market |
  DP, New Orleans Sq.

Royal St. Veranda |
  DP, New Orleans Sq.

CALIFORNIAN

La Brea | **DD**

☑ Napa Rose |
  DD, Grand Californian Hotel

Pacific Wharf Café |
  DCA, Golden State

☑ Storytellers Cafe |
  DD, Grand Californian Hotel

Vineyard Wine |
  DCA, Golden State

COFFEEHOUSES

Coffee House |
  DD, Disneyland Hotel

Surfside Lounge |
  DD, Paradise Pier Hotel

CREOLE

☑ Blue Bayou | DP, New Orleans Sq.
Café Orleans | DP, New Orleans Sq.
French Market | DP, New Orleans Sq.
☑ Ralph Brennan's | DD
Royal St. Veranda |
   DP, New Orleans Sq.

DESSERT

Baker's Field | DCA, Sunshine Plaza
Blue Ribbon Bakery | DP, Main St.
Bur-r-r Bank | DCA, Sunshine Plaza
Catch-a-Flave | DCA, Paradise Pier
Clarabelle's | DP, Toontown
Enchanted Cottage |
   DP, Fantasyland
Gibson Girl | DP, Main St.
Golden Horseshoe | DP, Frontierland
Häagen-Dazs | DD
La Brea | DD
Main St. Cones | DP, Main St.
Mint Julep | DP, New Orleans Sq.
Naples | DD
Plaza Inn | DP, Main St.
☑ Ralph Brennan's | DD
Royal St. Veranda |
   DP, New Orleans Sq.
Sam Andreas Shakes |
   DCA, Golden State
Tiki Juice Bar | DP, Adventureland

HEALTH FOOD

Bountiful Valley | DCA, Golden State
Critter Country Fruit |
   DP, Critter Country
Fairfax Fruit |
   DCA, Hollywood Pictures
Fantasyland Fruit | DP, Fantasyland
Farmer's Mkt. Fruit |
   DCA, Golden State
Jamba Juice | DD
Main St. Fruit | DP, Main St.
Pacific Wharf Café |
   DCA, Golden State

Schmoozies |
   DCA, Hollywood Pictures
Tomorrowland Fruit |
   DP, Tomorrowland
Tomorrowland Terr. |
   DP, Tomorrowland
Tropical Imports |
   DP, Adventureland
☑ Yamabuki |
   DD, Paradise Pier Hotel

HOT DOGS

Award Wieners |
   DCA, Hollywood Pictures
Corn Dog Castle |
   DCA, Paradise Pier
Little Red Wagon | DP, Main St.
Pluto's Dog Hse. | DP, Toontown

ICE CREAM PARLORS

Bur-r-r Bank |
   DCA, Sunshine Plaza
Catch-a-Flave | DCA, Paradise Pier
Gibson Girl | DP, Main St.
Häagen-Dazs | DD
Main St. Cones | DP, Main St.
Sam Andreas Shakes |
   DCA, Golden State
Tiki Juice Bar | DP, Adventureland

ITALIAN

Naples | DD
Napolini | DD
Pizza Oom Mow Mow |
   DCA, Paradise Pier
Wine Country Tratt. |
   DCA, Golden State

JAPANESE

☑ Yamabuki |
   DD, Paradise Pier Hotel

MEDITERRANEAN

☑ Catal | DD
Uva Bar | DD

MEXICAN

Cocina Cucamonga |
   DCA, Golden State
Rancho/Zocalo | **DP, Frontierland**
Rita's Baja | **DCA, Golden State**
Tortilla Jo's | **DD**
Tortilla Jo's Taqueria | **DD**

PIZZA

Daisy's Diner | **DP, Toontown**
Naples | **DD**
Napolini | **DD**

Pizza Oom Mow Mow |
   DCA, Paradise Pier
Z Redd Rockett's | **DP, Tomorrowland**

SEAFOOD

Hook's Pointe | **DD, Disneyland Hotel**

SOUTHERN

House of Blues | **DD**

STEAKHOUSES

Z Steakhouse 55 |
   DD, Disneyland Hotel

Dining Special Features

Listings cover the best in each category and include names and locations.

BRUNCH
House of Blues | DD
Ⓩ Ralph Brennan's | DD

BUFFET
(Check availability)
Disney's PCH Grill |
   DD, Paradise Pier Hotel
House of Blues | DD
Plaza Inn | DP, Main St.
Ⓩ Storytellers Cafe |
   DD, Grand Californian Hotel

DESSERT
Baker's Field | DCA, Sunshine Plaza
Blue Ribbon Bakery | DP, Main St.
Bur-r-r Bank | DCA, Sunshine Plaza
Catch-a-Flave | DCA, Paradise Pier
Clarabelle's | DP, Toontown
Enchanted Cottage | DP, Fantasyland
Gibson Girl | DP, Main St.
Golden Horseshoe | DP, Frontierland
Häagen-Dazs | DD
La Brea | DD
Main St. Cones | DP, Main St.
Mint Julep | DP, New Orleans Sq.
Naples | DD
Plaza Inn | DP, Main St.
Ⓩ Ralph Brennan's | DD
Royal St. Veranda |
   DP, New Orleans Sq.
Sam Andreas Shakes |
   DCA, Golden State
Tiki Juice Bar | DP, Adventureland

ENTERTAINMENT
(Call for days and times of
performances)
French Market | jazz |
   DP, New Orleans Sq.
Golden Horseshoe | revue |
   DP, Frontierland

House of Blues | varies | DD
Lost Bar | varies | DD, Disneyland Hotel
Ⓩ Ralph Brennan's | jazz | DD
Refreshment Corner | ragtime piano |
   DP, Main St.
Tomorrowland Terr. | varies |
   DP, Tomorrowland
Tortilla Jo's | mariachi | DD

LATE DINING
(Weekday closing hour)
Hearthstone | 1:45 AM |
   DD, Grand Californian Hotel
Lost Bar | 1:30 AM |
   DD, Disneyland Hotel

LOCAL FAVORITES
Ⓩ Blue Bayou |
   DP, New Orleans Sq.
Carnation Café | DP, Main St.
Ⓩ Catal | DD
ESPN Zone | DD
Hook's Pointe | DD, Disneyland Hotel
Little Red Wagon | DP, Main St.
Mint Julep | DP, New Orleans Sq.
Ⓩ Napa Rose |
   DD, Grand Californian Hotel
Naples | DD
Plaza Inn | DP, Main St.
Royal St. Veranda |
   DP, New Orleans Sq.
Ⓩ Steakhouse 55 |
   DD, Disneyland Hotel
Uva Bar | DD
Ⓩ Yamabuki | DD, Paradise Pier Hotel

MEET FOR A DRINK
Ⓩ Catal | DD
Cove Bar | DCA, Paradise Pier
Hearthstone |
   DD, Grand Californian Hotel

House of Blues | DD

Lost Bar | DD, Disneyland Hotel

🔁 Napa Rose |

   DD, Grand Californian Hotel

🔁 Ralph Brennan's | DD

🔁 Steakhouse 55 |

   DD, Disneyland Hotel

Surfside Lounge |

   DD, Paradise Pier Hotel

Tortilla Jo's | DD

Uva Bar | DD

Vineyard Wine | DCA, Golden State

Wine Cellar | DD, Disneyland Hotel

🔁 Yamabuki | DD, Paradise Pier Hotel

NOTABLE CHEFS

🔁 Catal | *Joachim Splichal* | DD

🔁 Napa Rose | *Andrew Sutton* |

   DD, Grand Californian Hotel

OUTDOOR DINING

(G=garden; P=patio; S=sidewalk;
T=terrace; W=waterside)

Café Orleans | P, W |

   DP, New Orleans Sq.

Carnation Café | P | DP, Main St.

🔁 Catal | T | DD

French Market | G |

   DP, New Orleans Sq.

Hungry Bear | P, W |

   DP, Critter Country

Naples | P | DD

Pacific Wharf Café | W |

   DCA, Golden State

Plaza Inn | P | DP, Main St.

🔁 Ralph Brennan's | T | DD

Rancho/Zocalo | P | DP, Frontierland

River Belle Terr. | P, S, W |

   DP, Frontierland

Stage Door Café | P, W |

   DP, Frontierland

Tomorrowland Terr. | T |

   DP, Tomorrowland

Tortilla Jo's | P | DD

Uva Bar | P | DD

Vineyard Wine | P |

   DCA, Golden State

Wine Country Tratt. | P |

   DCA, Golden State

PEOPLE-WATCHING

Café Orleans | DP, New Orleans Sq.

Carnation Café | DP, Main St.

🔁 Catal | DD

Cove Bar | DCA, Paradise Pier

Hearthstone |

   DD, Grand Californian Hotel

Hungry Bear | DP, Critter Country

La Brea | DD

Naples | DD

Royal St. Veranda |

   DP, New Orleans Sq.

Surfside Lounge |

   DD, Paradise Pier Hotel

Tomorrowland Terr. |

   DP, Tomorrowland

Tortilla Jo's | DD

Uva Bar | DD

Wine Country Tratt. |

   DCA, Golden State

QUICK BITES

Award Wieners |

   DCA, Hollywood Pictures

Baker's Field | DCA, Sunshine Plaza

Bengal BBQ | DP, Adventureland

Boudin Bread | DCA, Golden State

Bountiful Valley | DCA, Golden State

Captain's Galley |

   DD, Disneyland Hotel

Clarabelle's | DP, Toontown

Cocina Cucamonga |

   DCA, Golden State

Coffee House | DD, Disneyland Hotel

Corn Dog Castle | DCA, Paradise Pier

Critter Country Fruit |

   DP, Critter Country

Croc's Bits 'n' Bites |
  DD, Disneyland Hotel
Daisy's Diner | DP, Toontown
Enchanted Cottage |
  DP, Fantasyland
Fairfax Fruit |
  DCA, Hollywood Pictures
Fantasyland Fruit | DP, Fantasyland
Farmer's Mkt. Fruit |
  DCA, Golden State
Golden Horseshoe |
  DP, Frontierland
Hungry Bear | DP, Critter Country
Jamba Juice | DD
Little Red Wagon | DP, Main St.
Main St. Fruit | DP, Main St.
Mint Julep | DP, New Orleans Sq.
Napolini | DD
Pacific Wharf Café |
  DCA, Golden State
Pizza Oom Mow Mow |
  DCA, Paradise Pier
Pluto's Dog Hse. | DP, Toontown
Rancho/Zocalo | DP, Frontierland
⧗ Redd Rockett's |
  DP, Tomorrowland
Refreshment Corner | DP, Main St.
River Belle Terr. | DP, Frontierland
Royal St. Veranda |
  DP, New Orleans Sq.
Stage Door Café | DP, Frontierland
Studio Catering Co. |
  DCA, Hollywood Pictures
Taste Pilots' | DCA, Golden State
Tomorrowland Fruit |
  DP, Tomorrowland
Tomorrowland Terr. |
  DP, Tomorrowland
Toon Up Treats | DP, Toontown
Tortilla Jo's Taqueria | DD
Tropical Imports |
  DP, Adventureland
Village Haus | DP, Fantasyland

Wetzel's Pretzels | DD
White Water |
  DD, Grand Californian Hotel

QUIET CONVERSATION
⧗ Blue Bayou | DP, New Orleans Sq.
⧗ Catal | DD
Disney's PCH Grill |
  DD, Paradise Pier Hotel
Hearthstone |
  DD, Grand Californian Hotel
Hook's Pointe |
  DD, Disneyland Hotel
La Brea | DD
⧗ Napa Rose |
  DD, Grand Californian Hotel
⧗ Steakhouse 55 |
  DD, Disneyland Hotel
⧗ Storytellers Cafe |
  DD, Grand Californian Hotel
Surfside Lounge |
  DD, Paradise Pier Hotel
Vineyard Wine |
  DCA, Golden State
Wine Cellar | DD, Disneyland Hotel
Wine Country Tratt. |
  DCA, Golden State
⧗ Yamabuki |
  DD, Paradise Pier Hotel

ROMANTIC PLACES
⧗ Blue Bayou |
  DP, New Orleans Sq.
⧗ Catal | DD
⧗ Napa Rose |
  DD, Grand Californian Hotel
⧗ Steakhouse 55 |
  DD, Disneyland Hotel
Vineyard Wine |
  DCA, Golden State
Wine Cellar | DD, Disneyland Hotel
⧗ Yamabuki |
  DD, Paradise Pier Hotel

SPECIAL OCCASIONS

Z Blue Bayou | **DP, New Orleans Sq.**

Z Catal | **DD**

Z Napa Rose |
  DD, Grand Californian Hotel

Z Steakhouse 55 |
  DD, Disneyland Hotel

Z Storytellers Cafe |
  DD, Grand Californian Hotel

TEEN APPEAL

ESPN Zone | **DD**

Naples | **DD**

Z Rainforest Cafe | **DD**

Z Storytellers Cafe |
  DD, Grand Californian Hotel

Tomorrowland Terr. |
  DP, Tomorrowland

THEME RESTAURANTS

Z Blue Bayou | **DP, New Orleans Sq.**

ESPN Zone | **DD**

Golden Horseshoe | **DP, Frontierland**

Hook's Pointe | **DD, Disneyland Hotel**

House of Blues | **DD**

Z Rainforest Cafe | **DD**

Z Ralph Brennan's | **DD**

VIEWS

Z Blue Bayou | **DP, New Orleans Sq.**

Café Orleans | **DP, New Orleans Sq.**

Carnation Café | **DP, Main St.**

Z Catal | **DD**

Cove Bar | **DCA, Paradise Pier**

French Market | **DP, New Orleans Sq.**

Hook's Pointe | **DD, Disneyland Hotel**

Hungry Bear | **DP, Critter Country**

Z Napa Rose |
  DD, Grand Californian Hotel

Plaza Inn | **DP, Main St.**

Rancho/Zocalo | **DP, Frontierland**

River Belle Terr. | **DP, Frontierland**

Royal St. Veranda |
  DP, New Orleans Sq.

Stage Door Café | **DP, Frontierland**

Uva Bar | **DD**

Vineyard Wine | **DCA, Golden State**

Wine Country Tratt. |
  DCA, Golden State

WINNING WINE LISTS

Z Catal | **DD**

Hearthstone |
  DD, Grand Californian Hotel

Z Napa Rose |
  DD, Grand Californian Hotel

Uva Bar | **DD**

Vineyard Wine | **DCA, Golden State**

Wine Cellar | **DD, Disneyland Hote**

Wine Country Tratt. |
  DCA, Golden State

Shopping Merchandise

Includes store names and locations.

ACCESSORIES

Dinosaur Jack's |
   DCA, Paradise Pier

Disney Vault 28 | **DD**

Man Hat n' Beach | **DCA, Paradise Pier**

Parasol Cart | **DP, New Orleans Sq.**

Point Mugu | **DCA, Paradise Pier**

Royal St. Sweepers |
   DP, New Orleans Sq.

Silver Spur | **DP, Frontierland**

BOOKS

Compass Books | **DD**

☑ Off the Page |
   DCA, Hollywood Pictures

CAMERAS/VIDEO

Main St. Photo | **DP, Main St.**

CHILDRENSWEAR

Celebration Printers | **DP, Main St.**

Fly n' Buy | **DCA, Golden State**

Gone Hollywood |
   DCA, Hollywood Pictures

Greetings California |
   DCA, Sunshine Plaza

Once Upon a Time,
   The Disney Princess Shoppe |
   DP, Fantasyland

Rushin' River Outfitters |
   DCA, Golden State

Sideshow Shirts | **DCA, Paradise Pier**

Tower Hotel Gifts |
   DCA, Hollywood Pictures

☑ World of Disney | **DD**

COLLECTIBLES/
SOUVENIRS

Adventureland Bazaar |
   DP, Adventureland

Anne Geddes | **DD**

Autopia Winner's Circle |
   DP, Tomorrowland

Bonanza Outfitters | **DP, Frontierland**

☑ China Closet | **DP, Main St.**

Department 56 | **DD**

☑ Disneyana | **DP, Main St.**

Disney Showcase | **DP, Main St.**

Disney's Pin Traders | **DD**

☑ Emporium | **DP, Main St.**

Enchanted Chamber |
   DP, Fantasyland

Fantasy Faire Gifts | **DP, Fantasyland**

Gag Factory | **DP, Toontown**

Heraldry Shoppe | **DP, Fantasyland**

Houdini's Magic | **DD**

Indiana Jones Adventure Outpost |
   DP, Adventureland

Island Charters | **DD**

Le Bat en Rouge | **DP, New Orleans Sq.**

Le Petit Chalet | **DP, Fantasyland**

Little Green Men | **DP, Tomorrowland**

L' Ornement | **DP, New Orleans Sq.**

Mad Hatter | **DP, Fantasyland**

Mad Hatter Shop | **DP, Main St.**

Main St. Magic | **DP, Main St.**

Newsstand | **DP, Main St.**

Pieces of Eight | **DP, New Orleans Sq.**

Pioneer Merc. | **DP, Frontierland**

Pooh Corner | **DP, Critter Country**

Portrait Artists | **DP, New Orleans Sq.**

P.T. Flea Market | **DCA, Golden State**

☑ Silhouette Studio | **DP, Main St.**

Souvenir 66 | **DCA, Paradise Pier**

Star Trader | **DP, Tomorrowland**

Stromboli's Wagon |
   DP, Fantasyland

Tomorrowlanding | **DP, Tomorrowland**

Treasures in Paradise |
   DCA, Paradise Pier

Westward Ho | **DP, Frontierland**

Wishing Star | **DP, Fantasyland**

CRYSTAL

Cristal d'Orleans |
   DP, New Orleans Sq.

Crystal Arts | **DP, Main St.**

Wishing Star | **DP, Fantasyland**

HOME FURNISHINGS

Illuminations | **DD**

Market House | **DP, Main St.**

JEWELRY

☑ Jewel of Orleans |
   DP, New Orleans Sq.

New Century Jewel | **DP, Main St.**

MENS/WOMENSWEAR

(Stores carrying both)

Celebration Printers | **DP, Main St.**

Disney Clothiers LTD | **DP, Main St.**

Disney Vault 28 | **DD**

Fly n' Buy | **DCA, Golden State**

Gone Hollywood |
   DCA, Hollywood Pictures

Greetings California |
   DCA, Sunshine Plaza

Man Hat n' Beach |
   DCA, Paradise Pier

Quiksilver | **DD**

Rushin' River Outfitters |
   DCA, Golden State

Sideshow Shirts | **DCA, Paradise Pier**

South Sea Traders |
   DP, Adventureland

Tower Hotel Gifts |
   DCA, Hollywood Pictures

☑ World of Disney | **DD**

MUSIC/DVDS

20th Century Music Co. | **DP, Main St.**

PHOTOS/PORTRAITS

Amazing Pictures | **DD**

California Scream Cam |
   DCA, Paradise Pier

Kaman's Art | **DD**

Tom Kelly Caricatures | **DD**

SPECIALTY FOODS

☑ Candy Palace | **DP, Main St.**

Marceline's | **DD**

TOYS

☑ Build-a-Bear Workshop | **DD**

Engine Ears Toys |
   DCA, Sunshine Plaza

it's a small world | **DP, Fantasyland**

LEGO Imagination | **DD**

Midway Mercantile |
   DCA, Paradise Pier

Once Upon a Time,
   The Disney Princess Shoppe |
   DP, Fantasyland

Pioneer Merc. | **DP, Frontierland**

Rushin' River Outfitters |
   DCA, Golden State

Studio Store | **DCA, Hollywood Pictures**

WATCHES

Fortuosity Shop | **DP, Main St.**

Fossil | **DD**

ALPHABETICAL PAGE INDEX

Attractions

Dining

Hotels

Shopping

Character Dining

Disneyland.
RESORT

RESORT MAPS & PHOTOS

DISNEYLAND PARK
Date opened: **1955**
Size: **85 acres**
Architectural icon: **Sleeping Beauty Castle**

A"magical experience" for the "young at heart", this is the "classic" that "started it all" – and "Walt knew what he was doing when he designed" it; each of its eight "well-themed", "beautifully landscaped" lands exhibits "superb attention to detail", with "attractions for all ages" ranging from "timeless", "tried-and-true favorites" like the **Haunted Mansion** and **Pirates of the Caribbean** to such "recent must-sees" as the **Buzz Lightyear Astro Blasters** (and don't forget the "awesome" "parades, fireworks and **Fantasmic!**"); sure, the "crowds can be difficult to navigate", especially in summer, but most Mouseketeers find it's still "the Happiest Place on Earth."

DISNEY'S CALIFORNIA ADVENTURE

Date opened: **2001**
Size: **45 acres**
Architectural icon: **Grizzly Peak**

It "doesn't have the charm" (or crowds) of its "big brother", but there's "still a whole lot of fun to be had" at this "laid-back", "more grown-up" ode to the Golden State; pluses include "top-notch" attractions like the "amazing" **Twilight Zone Tower of Terror**, **Soarin' Over California** and new, "addictive" **Toy Story Midway Mania!**, as well as the "Broadway-style" **Aladdin** show, character dining at **Ariel's Grotto** and plentiful "liquid relief" (i.e. "wine and beer!"); still, critics gripe that there are too many "simple carnival rides" and "not enough to do for the money", though an ongoing "major rehab" aims to change that.

❶ TWILIGHT ZONE TOWER OF TERROR *California Adventure*

PROS: "hurl-rific" "head rush" "with random drops" that's "different every time"
CONS: "I started crying the one time I went on it" . . . "tamer than at WDW" . . . "not for small children"

❷ SPACE MOUNTAIN *Disneyland*

PROS: "classic coaster" . . . "dark thrill ride" with "curves tighter than my jeans from third grade"
CONS: "not for the faint of heart" . . . "wait is forever"

DISNEYLAND RESORT'S TOP 20 THRILLS

For full reviews, see the Park chapters

❸ CALIFORNIA SCREAMIN' *California Adventure*

PROS: "blasts off like a rocket" . . . "goes upside down through Mickey's face" . . . "fast and smooth"
CONS: "scared the bejabbers out of me" . . . "may leave you feeling dizzy"

❹ INDIANA JONES ADVENTURE *Disneyland*

PROS: "state-of-the-art dark ride" "packed with action and excitement" ("spiders, rats, fire, snakes")
CONS: "herky-jerky" . . . "long, tedious line" . . . "breaks down too much"

❺ SPLASH MOUNTAIN *Disneyland*

PROS: "wet fun on a hot Zip-a-Dee-Doo-Dah day" . . . "multiple drops" . . . "cute" "singing animatronics"
CONS: "don't go when it's cold outside!" . . . "can get pretty bumpy" . . . "takes a while to get interesting"

❻ GRIZZLY RIVER RUN *California Adventure*

PROS: "fast" . . . "guaranteed to get soaked" . . . "beautiful scenery"
CONS: "un-bear-able lines on a hot day" . . . "your shoes may fill up with water"

❼ MALIBOOMER* *California Adventure*

PROS: "shoots you straight up like a bullet" . . . "awesome view" "is worth every sweat bead" . . . "short lines"
CONS: "not for people afraid of heights" . . . "when I find my stomach, I'll let you know"   *will be removed in late 2009*

❽ MATTERHORN BOBSLEDS *Disneyland*

PROS: "still gives me a scare after 30 years" . . . "gotta love the yeti" . . . "listen to quality yodeling while waiting in line"
CONS: "bumpy ride, seating can be uncomfortable" . . . "effects are a bit old"

DISNEYLAND RESORT'S TOP 20 THRILLS
For full reviews, see the Park chapters

❾ BIG THUNDER MOUNTAIN RAILROAD *Disneyland*

PROS: "family-friendly", "rowdy good time"... "hang on to your hats and glasses (no, really, hang on!)"... "detailed scenery"
CONS: "your grandma's roller coaster"... "starting to show its age"

❿ SOARIN' OVER CALIFORNIA *California Adventure*

PROS: "eye-popping" "Imax meets flight simulator"... "see, hear and smell California"
CONS: "even the Fastpass line is crazy long"... "beware of motion sickness"

⑪ REMEMBER ... DREAMS COME TRUE FIREWORKS SPECTACULAR *Disneyland*

PROS: "amazing pyrotechnics" "perfectly timed to music" . . . "the show goes on all around you" . . . "never gets old" . . . "makes me cry every time!"
CONS: "can be canceled due to poor weather conditions" . . . "gets a little crowded"

⑫ TOY STORY MIDWAY MANIA! *California Adventure*

PROS: "4-D shooting gallery" . . . "I think I'm addicted" . . . "never a dull moment" . . . "easy for little hands to manipulate"
CONS: "your arm gets tired " . . . "wait time is a bummer" ("no Fastpass")

DISNEYLAND RESORT'S TOP 20 THRILLS
For full reviews, see the Park chapters

⑬ FANTASMIC! *Disneyland*

PROS: "spectacular" "visual feast for the eyes" . . . "see all of your favorite characters"
CONS: "may frighten small children" . . . "the longest wait in the West" . . . "get there early" "or you'll be watching the back of someone's head"

⑭ MULHOLLAND MADNESS *California Adventure*

PROS: "scarier than it looks" . . . "interesting theme" . . . "I've seen grown men brought to tears"
CONS: "a little hard on the body" . . . "wish it were longer" . . . "carnival coaster"

⓯ STAR TOURS *Disneyland*

PROS: "feels as if you're in a real spaceship" . . . "line is almost as interesting as ride itself"
CONS: "enough of Endor!" . . . "claustrophobic" . . . "don't go after lunch"

⓰ PIRATES OF THE CARIBBEAN *Disneyland*

PROS: "golden era classic" . . . "nice long ride" . . . "gets you out of the sun for a while" . . . "fun to find all of the Johnny Depps"
CONS: "beware of another catchy theme song" . . . "might frighten some small kids"

⓱ SUN WHEEL* *California Adventure*

PROS: "spectacular view" . . . "Ferris wheel with a twist" . . .
"out-of-control rocking sensation"
CONS: "boy, can it swing!" . . . "not for the squeamish" . . .
"slow loading time" *to be rethemed as Mickey's Fun Wheel in spring '09*

⓲ HAUNTED MANSION *Disneyland*

PROS: "Spooky, kooky" "tongue-in-cheek terror" . . . "cool
Nightmare Before Christmas makeover" . . . "newly redone
attic is perfect"
CONS: "little kids get scared" . . . "everything goes by so fast
you feel cheated" . . . ."theme song will run through your head
the rest of the day"

⑲ MAD TEA PARTY *Disneyland*

PROS: "always worth a spin" . . . "simple, absurd, stomach-churning fun" . . . "cute song, short line"
CONS: "round and round she goes, where you throw up, nobody knows" . . . "too short"

⑳ BUZZ LIGHTYEAR ASTRO BLASTERS *Disneyland*

PROS: "futuristic shooting gallery" is "like being inside a video game" . . . "e-mail your picture home for free" . . . "bragging rights"
CONS: "difficult to see where your laser is hitting"

DISNEYLAND RESORT'S HOTEL OVERVIEW
For full reviews, see the Downtown Disney chapter

DISNEY'S GRAND CALIFORNIAN HOTEL & SPA

PROS: "true escape" . . . "convenient to parks" . . . "breathtaking lobby"
CONS: "too expensive for me and my family to stay"

DISNEY'S PARADISE PIER HOTEL

PROS: "best room for the price" . . . "cute" "tropical theme"
CONS: "limited dining options" . . . "bit of a walk to the parks"

DISNEYLAND HOTEL

PROS: "friendly staff" . . . "family-oriented" . . . "excellent"
"pirate-themed pool"
CONS: "grande dame" "is showing its age"

BLUE BAYOU *Disneyland*

PROS: "amazing ambiance": "starry skies", "crickets chirp-ing", "Pirates of the Caribbean boats floating by"
CONS: "the price reflects the luxury"

WORLD OF DISNEY *Downtown Disney*

DINING & SHOPS

PROS: "everything Disney" — "if you can't find it here you're out of luck"
CONS: "you can get lost in this store!" . . . "gets super-crowded"

Disneyland RESORT

HOTELS
1. Disney's Grand Californian Hotel & Spa
2. Disney's Paradise Pier Hotel
3. Disneyland Hotel

THEME PARKS
4. Disneyland Park
5. Disney's California Adventure Park

AIRPORTS
6. John Wayne Airport - 13.5 miles from Disneyland Resort
7. Long Beach Airport - 20 miles from Disneyland Resort
8. Los Angeles International Airport - 34.5 miles from Disneyland Resort
9. Ontario International Airport - 35.5 miles from Disneyland Resort

OTHER
10. Downtown Disney District
11. Anaheim Convention Center